Speaking About
Money

Reducing the Tension

The
Giving Project

*Growing faithful stewards
in the church*

The Giving Project Series
A Christian View of Money: Celebrating God's Generosity
by Mark Vincent
Also available in Italian
Teaching a Christian View of Money: Celebrating God's Generosity
by Mark Vincent
A Christian View of Hospitality: Expecting Surprises
by Michele Hershberger
Also available in Chinese

Contact Mark L. Vincent
Telephone 1-219-320-3329
E-mail DesignForMinistry@Prodigy.net

Speaking About
Money

Reducing the Tension

Mark L. Vincent

Herald
Press

Scottdale, Pennsylvania
Waterloo, Ontario

Library of Congress Cataloging-in-Publication Data
Vincent, Mark.
    Speaking about money : reducing the tension / Mark L.
Vincent.
        p. cm.— (The giving project series)
    Includes bibliographical references and index.
    ISBN 0-8361-9147-1 (alk. paper)
    1. Stewardship, Christian. 2. Money—Religious aspects—
Christianity. I Title. II.
Series.

BV772.V57 2001
241'.68—dc21   2001024544

The paper used in this publication is recycled and meets the minimum requirements of American National Standard for Information Sciences—Permanence
of Paper for Printed Library Materials, ANSI Z39.48-1984.

SPEAKING ABOUT MONEY: REDUCING THE TENSION
Copyright © 2001 by Herald Press, Scottdale, Pa. 15683
    Published simultaneously in Canada by Herald Press,
    Waterloo, Ont. N2L 6H7. All rights reserved
Library of Congress Catalog Number: 2001024544
International Standard Book Number: 0-8361-9147-1
Printed in the United States of America
Book design by Jim Butti. Cover design by Merrill R. Miller

09 08 07 06 05 04 03 02 01   10 9 8 7 6 5 4 3 2 1

To order or request information,
please call 1-800-759-4447 (individuals),
1-800-245-7894 (trade). Website: www.mph.org

To Autumn and Zach,
for whom I always wish
a better way.

The Christian vocation is "to live into an ever-deepening and loving relationship with God." *Speaking About Money* is not another book about raising money. Through personal stories, probing questions, and practical guidelines Mark Vincent offers the faith community solid, basic, biblically sound, and spiritually inviting ways for individuals and congregations to grow in faithful stewardship. *Speaking About Money* says out loud what so many have felt: The deeper impulse of giving is worship. Stewardship is rooted in our experience of God's grace.

 —*Norma E. Wimberly, author, teacher and past director of Stewardship Education and Resource Development of the United Methodist Church, Nashville, Tennessee*

In *Speaking About Money: Reducing the Tension* Vincent's schemata for understanding the perspective folks have about money is new and particularly useful. Vincent acknowledges that churchly money conversations can be quickly sabotaged by anxiety, defensiveness or misunderstanding. Clear understandings of one's own perceptions and that of the group are significant leadership tools for reducing the tension when it arises. Those who lead money conversations will do well to gain this understanding through this resource. This book reiterates much of Vincent's helpful instruction in his earlier titles, *A Christian View of Money* and *Teaching a Christian View of Money.*

 —*Pam Peters-Pries, stewardship consultant with Mennonite Foundation of Canada, Blumenort, Manitoba*

Contents

Foreword

I heard it said that . . .

"Where there is no vision, the people perish.
Where there is no plan, the vision perishes.
Where there is no stewardship, the plan perishes."[1]

If true, then teaching and speaking about money and resource development should be a mentored program of study and practice for all leaders. Yet we live in a day when stewardship studies are offered in only a handful of theological schools, are not taught in Christian college classrooms or in the congregations across North America. Few believe in or see the spiritual connection between stewardship practice and discipleship growth as told by ancients and heroes of faith. This is why *Speaking About Money: Reducing the Tension* is so timely.

Permit me to give a further explanation of the crisis of need that we face for this resource. Today the study of stewardship is a diffuse movement. It is struggling to differentiate itself from traditional leadership studies. With the rise in nonprofit leadership education, and the reality that over 48% of all giving in North America go to religious causes, there has been a surge of interest in understanding the dynamics of giving. Coinciding with this interest is that in the last decade, over $20 million dollars has been spent in research to better comprehend the relationship of giving and philanthropy to nonprofit leadership. One would expect, with such an investment, to see numerous teaching resources as well as models of teaching, mentoring and speaking about stewardship readily available. Sadly, few have been developed. The majority of funded studies focus on giving trends and the negative results which show that we are now in the 29th year of decline in giving across North America.[2] Some have described the last ten years as a movement of curiosity in the study of stewardship.

Today, stewardship is a silent subject in need of fresh explanations and models of practice for a new age of leaders, set in a context in which they will understand and relate. As in any new movement, there are a variety of approaches to practice, from the sublime to the ridiculous. And at the moment, there are few authors that are positioning themselves to be the arbiters of legitimacy on the subject and practice of stewardship. Few have a handle on how to renew this interest.

Whether stewardship can once again become a meaningful concept and practice needs to be debated as well as researched. What we need today are models of how to teach this faith practice at the lay as well as leadership levels.

Speaking About Money: Reducing the Tension is that credible answer for today's leaders. Written in a style and format that is both personal and self-revealing, it will become one of a handful of reference works to turn to in our age of confusion on this subject. Better yet, this resource is designed to help leaders take a fresh look at their own images and form new models of stewardship, ones they can relate to and which will easily communicate to others.

In this guide leaders will find a theological basis of Christian beliefs about money, followed by an examination of perceptions about the same. Not limited to the style of traditional books that only speak to leaders, *Speaking About Money* will help its readers develop their own styles to carry forward the message as they also re-birth this almost lost practice and competence.

This title does not stop there. Its chapters on communicating the message for leaders, and the role of leaders in that process, are masterfully followed-up by resources for integrating new findings about stewardship through worship models. *Speaking About Money* is one of the most innovative works I have ever come across in my 15 years of steward leadership. And for such an important time as this.

I firmly believe that *Speaking About Money: Reducing the Tension* and its heralding predecessor, *A Christian View Of Money: Celebrating God's Generosity*, are two of the most important books written in the last 10 years. The information presented by their author, Mark L. Vincent, will, I believe, if heeded, become a most important compass to guide this next century's emerging faith leaders.

If you are a first-time reader, prepare to enter a new paradigm of speaking about money in your life first, and then in others. You will shortly be compelled to do so anew.

—*Scott Preissler, President*
Christian Stewardship Association
June 2001

Notes
1. Olan Hendrix, president—Leadership Resources Group
2. 1992 – 1996 Lilly Endowment funded CSA Parachurch Ministry Funding Project

Preface by the author

The myth says that money talk is a taboo. Not so. Money often shows up in our conversations, but in veiled ways. Instead of saying how much they spent on their vacation, a friend tells you where they went and what they did. You do a little covert math to figure out the cost. Instead of telling you the purchase price of the new car, your friend gives you a ride in it. The amount spent remains unexpressed, but it is not top secret information. A few inquiries and you can form reasonable estimates on how much money anyone earns and how they spend it. The taboo is doing the math, and if done, remaining silent about it.

Because we speak in such veiled ways, Christians are a little sensitive when money is the subject of public discourse, whether in preaching or in decision making. We don't mind saying how we are using money as we pursue recreation or provide a home, but when the amounts needed for ministry support get specific, or the Scripture text demands careful consideration of money use, our nervousness grows. When we give in to that nervousness, we avoid hearing what God wants to specifically address in our economic life. Do we trust in our income more than in God? What exactly do we look to for our salvation?

On top of this, a combination of money experiences and religious beliefs form our perceptions on the use of money by others, by the congregation, and how we hear the scriptural text. This unique mix of experience and belief sometimes interferes with the Christian community's ability to hear God in the middle of economic conversation. It also strikes fear in the heart of pastors who are called to preach the full counsel of God's word.

It was in a Kansas City steak house that the idea for a grid that mapped out money perceptions first took hold (see chart in chapter 4). I dined with David Miller, then a pastoral ministries instructor at Hesston (Kan.) College. I shared with him my vision to help pastors speak more effectively about money, and thereby apply faith to life. David suggested I find a way to chart how people viewed the same Scripture passages differently when they formed the theme of a worship service. He felt such a chart would help congregational leaders as they led in money matters. As David spoke, I sketched the concept on the back of a napkin and the grid was born.

Later, I showed my work to Orv Yoder, president of Mennonite Board of Education, Elkhart, Indiana, who suggested that we give each category unique names. Finally, Katherine Grusy, then an officer with Mennonite Foundation, Goshen, Indiana, organized a workshop where I could test these ideas with pastors and fundraisers for ministry organizations. Michele Hershberger and my wife, Lorie, both colleagues in *The Giving Project* offered much counsel and critique as I developed these ideas further.

These ideas became the basis of a seven-and-a-half-hour workshop, one component of a Giving Project

Gathering. For the last four years I was joined by Peter B. Wiebe, a consummate preacher and pastor, who taught the workshop with me. Many of our students encouraged us to put the contents of this workshop into the book you now hold in your hands. We asked Lani Wright to help us reduce our instruction to writing. We are grateful for the expertise and patience she brought to this process of stiching together my writing on the subject for the past five years and adding solid content along the way. I am also thankful to Ron and Lois Preheim and to Belmont Mennonite Church, Elkhart, Ind., for the resources in chapter 9 they helped to develop.

As you can see, a number of people deserve the credit for this material. I am grateful to them all, and hope I have not missed anyone. There are three whom I also want to especially thank. Each one is a model of effective preaching and teaching about money. They are Duane Yoder, Phil Kniss, and my own pastor, Duane Beck. Watching each of you perform gives me hope for the renewal of Christian witness in economic life.

—*Mark L. Vincent*
 Laurelville Mennonite Church Center
 Mount Pleasant, Pennsylvania

Introduction

Talk about money? You would be more likely to get the details of a neighbor's surgery than find out how much that same person makes or spent for their house. And it would be rude to ask! "In the domain of economic life," writes Sharon Daloz Parks, "we typically remain strangers to each other" *Practicing Our Faith: A Way of Life for a Searching People,* (Jossey-Bass, San Francisco, 1997, p. 47).

Christians aren't to be strangers to each other, but talking about money in church is almost considered more uncouth than talking about it on the sidewalk. Yet the church manages money all the time! Every time it is used, money illustrates values, confirms choices, and releases spiritual energy. To stay silent about money is to give it more power than it deserves—more power than God.

Speaking About Money is intended to help leaders break this silence. We will address such questions as: What assumptions can we make concerning beliefs about money? How are money perceptions formed? What are good ways to broach the subject? What types of giving impulses are driving people in congregations today? Here are four basic ways[1]:

1. Obligatory giving

Obligation sees giving and stewardship as a required offering or debt that needs to be paid. What remains is often separated from one's religious life and treated in secular ways. While giving may be done joyfully, the main purpose is to dutifully satisfy God. Stewardship as a result of religious obligation usually grows from outside the individual, and lacks strong internal motivation. The obliging steward may be most comfortable letting religious authorities decide how to use contributions. When taken to extremes, obligation leads people to find out the minimum requirements to appease God, to relieve guilt and fear, or so that they can expect divine blessing when they purchase it.

2. Philanthropy

Love (*phileo*) of man (*anthropos*) prompts the philanthropist to improve the social welfare of others. Those motivated by philanthropy respond to an ethical system. They think not so much about placating God as they aim to become a better person, by raising the quality of life in their neighborhood or world, by returning some of the good things of life they received so that others may share in them, or by adding beauty to the world.

Stewardship through philanthropy is far more individualistic than stewardship by obligation. Philanthropists are free to pursue their own interests, to follow their gifts, to withhold giving, or to grant it based on their satisfaction with the way the money is used. At the extreme, however, philanthropy results in a giving without true generosity. Gifts can be given with strings attached, usually intertwined with the giver's concern about their own well-being, their sense of satisfaction, or even their legacy.

3. Prosperity

Prosperity-driven stewardship is as ancient as Yahweh's material promises to the patriarchs Abraham, Isaac, and Jacob. Honor Yahweh, and you will be rewarded with large families and material prosperity. The newly freed Hebrews staked their hopes on Yahweh's promise that honoring the covenant would result in material blessing (Deuteronomy 28).

A prosperity view of stewardship produces the most consistent, disciplined, and generous givers. Taught and reinforced by the community, individual households make their gifts believing God holds untold material wealth and spiritual blessing just for them. For some, this form of stewardship becomes a sort of divine brokerage house—investment is made with a God who then returns it with interest.

4. A deeper impulse: Worship

The obligation, philanthropy, and prosperity perspectives are based on some form of entitlement. Obligation purchases a greater degree of security. From the philanthropy angle, all people are entitled to share in the assets that both creation and economy provide. Sharing entitles one to be viewed as a good, generous, and respectable person. A nice bonus is a return on the investment in a divine enterprise. Prosperity counts on God who never breaks a promise. Therefore one can expect divine blessing from the God who said that blessings would come.

In spite of all that is good—even biblical—about these three perspectives, there remains a deeper religious impulse for stewardship—that of worship. It is a stewardship rooted in an experience with grace that branches out into a worshipful response. In short, this response can be expressed by the phrase: *Generous God, generous life.* The person who encounters the saving power of Christ is motivated by a response deeper than obligatory tithing, goodwill toward others, or seeking more of God's blessings. It leads to a whole life commitment, a burning desire to help others know the fullness of life God intends. Stewardship through worship is no longer something you *do*, it is something you *become*. This steward organizes life so God can give them away.

Who is a steward?

A steward is a special kind of servant. She or he is trusted to take care of someone else's assets. These assets can be property, equipment, wealth, or even people. Stewards are servants who treat their charges as if they were their own. There are dozens of reasons we may feel gratitude and be prompted to return a favor. The stewardship spark is ignited when we know we hold a trust that was never entirely ours, and that this trust will be passed to others when we are finished. Although faith is not needed to experience the wonder that leads to a stewardship response, religious faith does broaden and deepen the impulse.

So how do we develop this response in our people? How can we make sure this is the root for our own stewardship? This book is full of strategies that will assist church leaders in doing these things.

Notes

1. For more about this topic see, *A Stewardship Manifest* by Mark Vincent © 2000. A free document is available from www.givingproject.net

PART I

Christian beliefs about money

Money works. Money talks. Every time money is used it illustrates values, confirms choices, and releases spiritual energy. Whatever we do, we give witness as to who we are.

Take Michele's parents, for example. They are real entrepreneurs, who own their own gasoline, diesel, and propane gas business. While they make money some would say that their business practices are "deplorable."

Michele's parents never deny propane to a user in the winter, no matter how high the customer's debt. They report their inventory accurately on the tax records, even though it would be easy to lie. They close down their gas stations on Sundays, despite pressure from their supplier to stay open. They lend out personal vehicles to their customers, whose cars are in the shop, even though they have had one stolen that way. They do whatever it takes to pay a customer back if there is a miscalculation of the charge.

Furthermore, Michele's parents do not worry. If the accounts-receivable ledger is sky high, it's okay, because God will take care of them. If there aren't enough funds to pay for the new load of propane, it's okay. God is in control of their business. Through threat of bankruptcy and million-dollar successes, Michele's parents do not worry.

It pays off spiritually. Because of who they are with their money, people have begun a relationship with

Jesus. Because of their generosity and contentment, with or without money, people want to know more. They can see the honesty, as well as the freedom from worry, and they want the same thing. Michele's parents not only use their money with integrity; they also lead people to the source of their integrity. [1]

What values and energy does your money release?

Notes

1. Portions of this introduction were written by Michele Hershberger and were first published in *Generous Living*, June 1997. To receive your free copy of this monthly e-mail helpsheet, please send your request and e-mail address to stewardship@mma-online.org

CHAPTER 1

Christian beliefs about money

Most believers can express basic Christian under-standings about communion, marriage, or the importance of God's word. They struggle, however, to articulate faith understandings about money in a consistent and non-anxious way. How can we help newcomers and youth readily identify and embrace our beliefs about money? How can we encourage long-standing Christians to become more articulate about these beliefs? We want to place these beliefs at the very heart of our faith, because the linkage between faith and practice runs as a strong current through North American wallets. We want to preserve and increase our faithful use of money so we can better represent the generosity of Christ to a hurting world.

God is God and money is not

There is nothing that competes so intensely for our attention toward God as money. Although money is only a tool, it has a godlike power. Money can eclipse all other priorities. While we can choose whether we will use our money for good or for ill, we must first choose whether or not money will rule us.

Our culture insists that we think about money—how

we will earn it, how we will spend it, and whether we have enough of it. Since money is such a dominant force, our faithfulness to the way of Jesus includes our actions with money. This is why Christians need to articulate their beliefs about money. Our beliefs are:

- Because money has a godlike strength, our earning and use of money communicate our values.
- Christians are citizens of a society God is building and are called to share God's values—that is to view and respond to the world the way God does.
- God's values all culminate in this: restoring the universe to its intended purpose—a place of abundant life, a place without suffering, a place where people get to enjoy the fruits of their labor, a place without oppression, or death, or grief, or poverty. Christians respond by giving our life's work to God's service, and to using money to help God provide abundant life for all.
- Jesus, as our Christ and Lord of the universe, is where we meet God's generosity. When we meet this grace in Jesus, we are empowered to live out our belief that God is Owner of all. Jesus is our best example of how to live out these values.
- We embrace Jesus as the Christ and Lord of the universe, and dedicate all of life to him and want to help God build this new society.
- We demonstrate this dedication by giving back to God out of the first and best of all we've been given, and manage the rest in generous ways that give glory to God.
- Given money's power and the constant temptation to move away from a whole life dedication, we need the Holy Spirit and the church family to help us be accountable. Our best decisions about living

generously are made with the help of other people seeking to be fully dedicated to God.[1]

The following diagram lays out these beliefs in sequence:

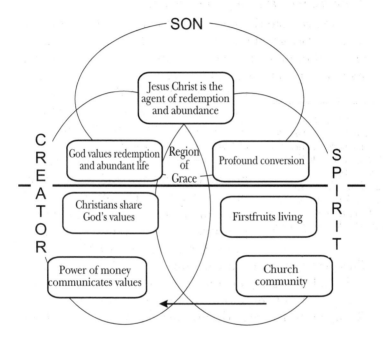

- Please note the "Region of Grace" in the diagram. Our life with money must pass through this region or we are not able to make worship the source of our stewardship. Without doing so, we will continue to use obligation, philanthropy, or prosperity as our stewardship fuel.

These beliefs are either passed on or undermined in the language and activities of the congregation. There are also seven avenues for helping congregations live out their beliefs about money. They include [2]

1. Preaching/teaching about money

Money, materialism, and consumption have godlike powers. Pastors, elders, deacons, and other church leaders need to have an adequate grasp of a Christian belief system about money, and be aware how it impacts their own lives. These leaders start with a money autobiography (see chapter 2), through which they tell their life stories around money.

"All our time, talents, and money in the church belong to God's great mission of restoring the creation to its full, fruitful function."—Walter Bruggemann in *Using God's Resources Wisely: Isaiah and Urban Ministry.* (1993, Westminster John Knox Press)

They also use a variety of resources to preach and teach about money with more authority, and more often. This book will help people preach more money *applications* instead of more stewardship *sermons.*

This guide provides instructions for leading the church as it makes money decisions, as well as a rationale for being aware of the giving patterns of church members. Giving patterns are a window into one's spiritual walk.

2. Dedicating offerings

Many congregations *take* the offering instead of *receiving* it. In worship the offering is used as a commercial break instead of a sacramental act. At best it is an unthinking ritual to meet the church budget. We make a quick prayer over it and cover the collection with churchy background music. At worst, the offering has no connection at all to why we gather to worship God. We do it just because that is what you do at church.

Get acquainted with resources for *receiving* an offering. Make it a weekly worship celebration where we offer the first and best of our incomes along with our talents and our time. Worship leaders can learn to dedicate an offering, to lift it up to God and offer it as a response to God's grace. Consider carefully *where* to place the offering in the order of worship. How can we use the offering as a reminder of our beliefs about Christians and money? How can we create a relationship between the gift-giver and the gift-receiver in worship?

See chapter 7 for more ideas on how to dedicate offerings.

3. Congregational ministries of mercy

Most congregations engage in some form of mercy ministry. At the very least, the pastor responds to emergency calls, or when sickness and death occur in a family. Many churches, however, have chosen to be proactive and lay-led in their mercy ministry. Congregations appoint key members as eyes and ears for the church. Their role is to identify needs, link them to available resources, and invite other congregational members to lend their gifts and skills. These "point people" also network with mutual aid societies, financial planners, church treasurers, and pastors for additional resources.

But mercy ministry—responding to physical and material needs within the congregation and local community—must also plan for meeting needs *before* they become a crisis. How?

- Check in on people at critical stages of life. Form a system in which every person in the congregation receives attention that focuses around special or stressful events. There can be a special celebration for youth when they receive a driving license or graduate from high school. College students appreciate pastoral counsel about career choices, visits on campus, as well as care packages. Offer money management courses geared to the needs of young adults, the newly retired, and seniors. Singles ministries, grief counseling, dedications for new homes or businesses, and workshops for empty-nesters can supplement the traditional bridal and baby showers.

- Mercy ministries benefit from **lay leadership**. The pastor can't and shouldn't do it all. Having other "ministers" who hold primary responsibility for mercy allows pastors to focus on prayer, spiritual direction, and scriptural instruction. Pastors need to be involved in caregiving, by supplementing instead of initiating the care. This frees them for other aspects of their ministry. Likewise, lay members need to be empowered to use their God-given gifts of mercy. Spreading around the blessing is the deep satisfaction that comes with mercy ministry.

4. Connecting givers to receivers

It is no secret that people have become quite concerned about where their donated dollars go. This might stem from the fact that when people talk about giving their money, they forget that all of life is dedicated to God.

It is not a matter of being selfish. Scandals among television evangelists and fundraising scams make people more wary. They want to be sure their offerings really do honor God. So they try to keep those offerings close to home, where they can see that their money is used for its intended purposes. When a person discovers an opportunity to help someone, it creates a more profound bond than when the committee extends mercy. Try to put human faces on the dollars contributed by the congregation. Stress that we are all ministers, all of us are called to reach out to others.

- **Gather a reference group** to help you think about faith to life applications growing out of a Scripture text. Invariably a number of them will relate to one's participation in the economy. A constant pitfall for the preacher is to apply the text only to the life of the congregation, a setting in which the Christian only spends a small fraction of time. By making application to one's life as a consumer, investor, family member, wage earner, and real estate broker, preaching becomes both more relevant and powerful.

- **Tell stories**. Make time in the worship service for telling stories of ministry. The interview format is one effective way to do this. Remember that the stories may include giving money, possessions, as well as many other types of gifts.

- **Participate in the 40-Day Experiment**. Challenge your congregation to pray this prayer every day for the next 40 days, "God, please send someone for me to minister to today." This life-changing exercise will help the participants see God's hand in the ordinary situations in their lives. Provide time in the worship service for people to report the ways God answered their prayers. Encourage them to use each other and the Holy Spirit for support when their ministry seems overwhelming.[3]

5. Living a firstfruits lifestyle

Identify the first and best that belongs to God. Start by having the spiritual leadership of the church—the pastor, elders, deacons, *and* their spouses—write a money autobiography and seek God's direction for the gifts they offer back to God. Send these money-renewal ripples into the congregation. These leaders can then work with The Giving Project[4] to host additional retreats until at least 75 percent of the congregational membership participates.

Host a workshop that connects planned giving to the Old Testament jubilee celebration. Study the Christian belief system about money (see *A Christian View of Money*). This strategy is the most comprehensive and difficult one to complete. It is also the one most likely to bring spiritual renewal to your congregation.

6. *Transferring leadership between generations of Christians*

Every experienced person was once a novice. Experience was gained because someone gave the person opportunities and encouragement in both success and failure. The gift of opportunity is also a gift of gaining ownership. When someone feels ownership in a ministry, he or she is far more likely to invest personal energy (schedule, expertise, and funds), and invite others to come along.

Build leadership cultivation into the very fabric of congregational life. Promote respect between generations. *No one has really led until he or she has successfully trained someone to fill her or his shoes.* Congregations that want to develop a community of committed, dedicated, and generous Christians know how important it is to develop the next generation of Christians. Improve the assimilation of new members by paying special attention to the ministry of hospitality.

Do the generations need different worship settings because of their unique needs and experiences? Church growth analyst Lyle Schaller reports that it is rare to find people above 70 and under 30 in the same worship service. Rare, but not impossible. The future holds our Christian hope so we need not be frightened of it. God stands at the end of our time on earth with arms outstretched to receive us. Congregations who live by this assurance find fewer reasons to worry about the responses of the different generations. Though some might advocate a particular worship style, or someone else might want to update electronic technology[5], as a whole they harbor a passionate commitment to develop the gifts of other people. Then younger Christians eagerly listen for wisdom from those who have more experience, and "elders" enthusiastically give younger and newer folk permission to try their wings and fly.

Leadership transfer between generations of Christians involves passing on values. These values are a trust that the next generation manages for those who will follow them. Since stewardship is about managing the resources of God's creation, it includes wise management of the people God loves so much. Instead of feeling anxious that what we have worked to build will disappear, we look forward to others building on the foundation we have laid.

7. Managing congregational finances

The kinks in any congregational system seem to show up when the church discusses money. Some congregations need to train their people in good committee process in order to fix the decision-making system. That makes monetary decisions more effective. Also, churches need to establish a congregational mission statement with clear goals.

Other related financial tasks may include: establishing a reserve fund, developing and using budget ratios to guide the planning process, committing to a percentage of giving outside the congregation, and inviting the congregation to estimate their giving on an annual basis. These tools, along with linking the congregation's mission to proactive financial planning, can fund a ministry that the church looks *forward* to rather than funding last year's program all over again.

The call of God is to live expansively. That's not the same as living expensively. "Being good stewards is impossible when we're trying to be big owners," preaches Pastor Ben Dake. Our main job as Christians is **to live into an ever-deepening and loving relationship with God**—John Westerhoff's version of the classic catechetical answer to the meaning of life. God doesn't want us to make a difference in this world, but to "*live in the difference God has already made.*" Our prayer is not "God, tell me what I should do," but "God, what are you doing, and how can I cooperate?" God's work is already accomplished. Now God is waiting for *us* to arrive. Living into this work fuels our generosity, stokes our evangelistic efforts, and keeps programs as well as bricks and mortar as tools of service rather than the ends of ministry. This keeps the church alive for the next generation.

"Advertisements coax us to buy, to possess, and to accumulate more—but even worse, they convince us that in buying, possessing, and accumulating more, we ourselves actually become more. The latest DVD player, television, automobile, or designer clothing is presented as the answer to sagging self-esteem, troubled relationships, and loneliness. Without the latest expensive belongings, we feel inferior and begin to believe that we are nothing. With them, we think more highly of ourselves and find our identity restored. Having said yes to the acquisition of so many material things, we are unable to say yes to the larger demands of the Spirit. Slowly, perhaps even bitterly, we come to realize that we do not own our possessions, they own us.

—M. Shawn Copeland, "Saying Yes and Saying No," in *Practicing Our Faith: A Way of Life for a Searching People* (p. 64, 1997, Jossey-Bass, San Francisco).

Notes

1. For an in-depth treatment of these beliefs read *A Christian View of Money: Celebrating God's Generosity*, by Mark Vincent (1999, Herald Press, Scottdale, Pa.).

2. For an in-depth treatment of these seven avenues, along with numerous resources for action, see the manual *Teaching a Christian View of Money: Celebrating God's Generosity*, by Mark Vincent (1997, Herald Press, Scottdale, Pa.).

3. To learn more about the 40-day experiment, see the book *A Christian View of Hospitality: Expecting Surprises* (1999, Herald Press, Scottdale, Pa.).

4. Contact: Mennonite Mutual Aid, Stewardship Education Center, P.O. Box 483, Goshen, IN 46527, Attn.: Steven R. Granger. 1-800-348-7468, fax: 219-533-5264, e-mail: stewardship@mma-online.org.

5. See Mark Vincent, "Feasibility questions for purchasing technology," a downloadable document from www.DesignForMinistry.com. Available January 2002.

CHAPTER 2

Your life with money (money autobiography)

Money is a universal language, but sometimes we don't know how to speak it. Go ahead! Talk about it! Tell stories about it! Who taught you to manage money? How was/is money discussed in your family? How was/is money discussed in your church? What is your current money situation? What are your financial goals? Where did we get our information (about money)? How did our parents spend money? What is the first echo from their habits to your life that you remember?

Church renewal in managing resources must start with the leaders. Pastors, elders, deacons, and others need to tell their life stories around money. Money questions in the congregation must be addressed by the spiritual leadership, simply because money is such a powerful force. Don't be silent! Don't skip this step in your plan for congregational renewal!

Church leaders need to be offered healing, hope, and accountability when anger, fear, pain, and sin come to the surface. Once they are renewed, they can lead church members in a similar experience until the congregation faces its relationship with money. Denominations need to provide adequate support systems for pastors and congregations who are trying to break out of tired patterns, as well as model faithful and mature management practices.

Congregations begin this money storytelling through a weekend retreat for their spiritual leadership. Following the event, congregational leaders work with a Giving Project consultant to lead similar experiences for members of the congregation. A retreat format is the best way to help people tell their money stories. Retreats pull people away from the routines of family, work, and church. This helps them prepare for greater openness and fuller participation.

Money autobiography retreat

Rosemary Williams, a certified financial planner and former staff member for Ministry of Money, designed the worksheet on the next page to help people walk through a money autobiography. Ask participants to answer these questions in writing or by recording on a cassette tape before the retreat begins. Indicate that they need to answer only the questions with which they are comfortable. They may add additional dimensions as they wish.

Family History	**Present Family**
1. Who were your money management role models?	1. Who are your current money management role models?
2. Who handled the money in your family?	2. Who handles the money?
3. How did they handle the money?	3. How do they handle the money?
4. Was money discussed in your family?	4. Is money easily discussed?
5. Was the money supply abundant/scarce?	5. Is the money supply abundant/scarce?

Current Family Financial Facts

Annual Income:	Current Needs:
Annual Expenses:	Current Wants:
Assets (I own):	Current Giving: How much money will pass through my hands in the next:
Liabilities (I owe):	10 years _____?
	20 years _____?

Net Worth:
How much money has
passed through my hands in
the last:

10 years _____?

20 years _____?

A suggested schedule for a money autobiography retreat

Friday	Saturday	Sunday
7:00 p.m.	8:00 a.m.—	8:00 a.m. —
• Gather	• Gather	• Gather
• Introductions and conversation about expectations of the retreat.	• Breaking the silence	• Breaking the silence
• Singing	• Words of hope/prayer	• Words of hope/prayer
• Devotional	• Breakfast	• Breakfast
• More singing		
• Input *(Each input session during the retreat features a participant or other person's life story around money.*	9:00 a.m.—	9:00 a.m.—Small groups
	• Singing	
	• Input	11:00 a.m.—
These might be done in person, via video or audio recording.	10:00-12:00 noon—Small groups	• Singing
		• Worship service that includes the following elements:
Stories should come from a variety of people in many situations. Pay attention to the people who are coming and the style of input to which each responds best.)	12:00 noon— Lunch	1. Worship center for symbols that represent what participants want to give to God.
	1:00-2:30 p.m.— Break	2. Communion
		3. Anointing for those who request it.
	2:30 p.m.—	
	• Singing	
	• Input	
• Small-group assignments	3:30-5:30 p.m.— Small groups	12:00 noon— Lunch/Depart
9:30 p.m.— Depart in silence	5:30 p.m.—Dinner	
	7:30 p.m.—	
	• Singing	
	• Input	
	9:00 p.m.—Depart in silence	

Notes on the money autobiography weekend:

- Remember that consultants are ready to help you with planning and leadership of the retreat.
- It is possible for a number of congregations to share in this weekend.
- Strongly encourage spouses to participate. Provide childcare so this can happen.
- An alternative to planning your own retreat is to participate in events hosted by Ministry of Money. For information and dates contact: Ministry of Money 11315 Neelsville Church Road, Germantown, MD 20876, 301-428-9560, fax 301-428-9573, e-mail: office@ministryofmoney
- The importance of holding this retreat right cannot be overstated. Put your best energies and resources into it. This is the basic building block out of which grows the rest of the process for congregational change.

CHAPTER 3

Money messages

She showed up at a crowded, swanky restaurant, and was politely informed that without a reservation, seating would be impossible. The woman slipped a bill to the maître d', and, miraculously, a table became available. She took her place with a satisfied smirk.

You have seen that scene time and again in person and in movies. It may be frustrating that money seems to be the only voice that can command results for some people. But money also talks in another way. It shouts out what we value. It's better than a bumper sticker or vanity license plate. Each time we make a purchase, decide on an investment, or give a gift, we communicate what we care about. In his book *Women, Men and Money: The Four Keys to Using Money to Nourish Your Relationship, Bankbook, and Soul,* William Devine Jr. (1998, Crown Publishing Group) includes a series of helpful tables that match actions with the messages they convey. The following are a few examples, both positive and negative:

- **Message given:** Your partner wants to quit his job. You say, "To do what? That's all you know."
- *Message received*: Others can flourish, but I doubt that you can.
- **Message given:** Seeing what good the physical therapy does after elbow surgery, you suggest that your spouse arrange for some extra appointments, even

though the health insurance will not cover any more visits and you will have to pull the money out of the retirement fund.

- *Message received*: Let's get you healthy, and then we'll figure out how to earn more money.
- **Message given:** You tell your accountant or mechanic that you want to pay her under an odd arrangement, or you complain about her fees even though you say you want to work with her.
- *Message received*: I want your work, but I don't want to pay you. Taking me on as a client will be painful.
- **Message given:** Your offer to buy a house includes the proposal to put a 10 percent deposit into escrow immediately upon acceptance.
- *Message received*: Even though I will get these funds back if the deal does not close, I want you to know I am serious about the deal.
- **Message given:** Many of your financial decisions are tax-driven.
- *Message received*: I'm not calling the shots in my life. The government tax agency is.
- **Message given:** You spend money to upgrade your stereo system in your car, rather than pay the rent on time.
- *Message received*: My pleasure is more important than my reliability.
- **Message given:** Though you can ill afford to set aside more than your regular tithe, you put up the first money for a down payment fund to purchase a house your congregation is buying to host refugees.
- *Message received*: I'm committed to this ministry.

Devine's advice is not to squander money, but to make it speak your language, make it do justice to your values. "Transactions speak louder than words," he writes. This is not a new concept, but talking about money openly enough to help each other live what we speak is tough.

While parts of Devine's book are very helpful, it does not take into consideration the Christian vocation: **to live into an ever-deepening and loving relationship with God.** Christians are called to share God's values—that is, to view and respond to the world the way God does. Therefore we want the use of our money to line up with God's values.

In Isaiah's vision of God's new society we catch a glimpse of what God wants to provide to all humanity. The believer's worldview is to be entwined with God's agenda in order to restore the universe.

God's New Society (Isaiah 65:17-25)

Isaiah describes God's new society as:

Happy (Isaiah 65:17-19).
- God commands eternal gladness and rejoicing in the new creation (v. 18).
- The people who live there are a joy to behold (v. 18).
- The newly created Jerusalem brings delight. Weeping and crying are removed (v. 19).

Healthy (Isaiah 65:20).
Infant mortality disappears. Citizens of the new society enjoy complete and expanded life expectancies. To dream of a society where children do not die, where disease is absent, and where righteousness is rewarded with long life, is to picture paradise.

Just (Isaiah 65:21-22).

God creates a society where land is fairly distributed, where people can live in the homes they build, and in which nobody fills their bellies with crops forcibly taken from another. Justice, especially with land use, is a value God created within this new society.

Full of dignity (Isaiah 65:22-24).

The society God intends to create also grants dignity to people. God says, "My chosen ones will long enjoy the works of their hands. They will not toil in vain or bear children doomed to misfortune; for they will be a people blessed by the Lord, they and their descendants with them. Before they call I will answer; while they are still speaking I will hear."

- The society God creates provides fulfilling work for its citizens. There are no unfair labor practices. Nobody gets forced into jobs that destroy their dignity.
- People shall not labor as slaves for another, with no hope for the well being and dignity of their descendants.
- Those who try to seek God in this life often find communication hindered, but in God's new society all hindrances are removed.

Peaceful (Isaiah 65:25).

Natural enemies in the animal kingdom become the best of friends. Carnivores become herbivores. Dangerous serpents become harmless as house pets. God's new society is peaceful.

The Bible sends many messages about God's vision for human society. Isaiah's description is only one of these. Wealth and prosperity, monetary and otherwise, is part of that vision. Another is the story of creation, and the assertion that we are made in God's image. The use of money is a creative way we demonstrate that we are made in God's image. Does our use of money line up with God's values? Does it reveal God's image?

It's fairly clear that how we use money sends messages *about* us. But what messages does your use of money send *to you*? Can we ask ourselves these pointed questions?

1. Does our use of money nurture the image of God within us?
2. Does it enhance the promise inherent in our creation?
3. Are you making your money to nourish you as you live for God's vision, or are you allowing it to exploit you because you fear society's harsh rules and judgment more than God's?
4. Does your use of money nurture that creative fire in your belly, or does it douse it with messages of financial doom?

Try this exercise

List three money decisions you must make in the next week. Next to each one, record the message that the person receiving the money will receive from you.

1. Decision

   Message

2. Decision

Message

3. Decision

Message

Does your earning and use of money:
- show that you rejoice in creation?
- nurture the divine promise within you?
- foster true joy for you and others?
- help create a just distribution of economic resources?
- promote peace in God's new society?
- grant dignity to people?
- help people enjoy complete and expanded life expectancies?
- provide fulfilling work for you and others?

If not, what will you change to correct your behavior?

PART II

Perceptions about money

Would you pay four dollars for fresh squeezed lemonade? Would you after walking eight blocks in 108-degree heat? Would you if you were on an expense account of your employer? Would you if there were no drinking fountains? Even then, four dollars seems steep.

The high-priced refreshment booth also sold iced tea for a lower price. I went for the tea. While the proprietor filled my order, I asked how business was that day.

"I'm getting a lot of remarks about my prices," she said. "It's a religious event so I'll be lucky to recover my costs. My chief income comes during business-related events. People who spend their company's money don't blink an eye at my prices."

She proceeded to give me an economics lesson on lemonade stands at convention centers. First, there was an annual proprietor's license and city regulations on quality of equipment. Then there was a 15 percent commission on all sales to be paid to the convention center. She hired one or two part-time employees to staff the 16-hour days, and finally there were the related expenses of being an employer. She did not mention the price of lemons, ice, and cups.

I did some math in my head. If I wanted to own my own lemonade stand in a convention center, giving it my full-time effort, how much money would I want to earn? How many days a week would I need to work? How many glasses of lemonade would I need to sell on a given day?

Suddenly four dollars did not sound like much. Suddenly I was more sympathetic. Perspective expands when we take a little time to listen. I won't necessarily purchase more four-dollar lemonades on hot days, but I will be nicer to those who sell it.

CHAPTER 4

How people construct money perceptions

Money is a universal power. It is also a universal language. We use money as consumers (grocery store), investors (stocks, real estate, education), workers, and as worshipers.

The church is the distribution center for our worship gifts to God. Money speaks for us, expresses our values. As youngsters we take our clues from family members (including the church family) about how to think about, talk about, and manage money.

The Bible provides guidance about the appropriate use of money. Because we are made in God's image, we take behavioral cues from what we read in the biblical stories. When we need to use money, it helps to keep in the forefront of our minds God's tick list of values. Isaiah describes God's desirable new society as **happy** (Isaiah 65:17-19), **healthy** (Isaiah 65:20), **just** (Isaiah 65:21-22), **full of dignity** (Isaiah 65:22-24), and **peaceful** (Isaiah 65:25). We want to line up our values with God's values, and use money accordingly.

Why give?

There are three main motivations for giving. Alone, none is completely adequate.

1. Philanthropy: "Because I care about the welfare of others, I'll give." This Christian philanthropist finds motivation in the cross of Jesus. The cross invites the philanthropist to minister to the world's needs so the work of God gets done and God's kingdom becomes visible. The hymn "Lift High the Cross" expresses this motivation.

Refrain
Lift high the cross, the love of Christ proclaim
till all the world adore his sacred name.

Verses
1. O Lord, once lifted on the tree of pain,
draw all the world to seek you once again.

2. From north and south, from east and west,
we raise in growing unison our song of praise.

3. Let ev'ry race and ev'ry language tell
of him who saves our lives from death and hell.

4. Set up your throne, that earth's despair may
cease beneath the shadow of its healing peace.

George W. Kitchin, 1887; revised by Michael R.
Newbolt, 1916, alt.
© 1974 Hope Publishing Co., Carol Stream, IL 60188
All rights reserved. Used with permission

2. Discipleship: "Because Jesus set this example, I want to do it too." The discipleship oriented Christian sees sacrificial giving as following the example of Jesus in giving all. A hymn related to this perspective is: "When We Walk with the Lord (Trust and Obey)"

Refrain

Trust and obey, for there's no other way
to be happy in Jesus, but to trust and obey.

Verses

1. When we walk with the Lord in the light of his
   word,
what a glory he sheds on our way!
While we do his good will, he abides with us still,
and with all who will trust and obey.

2. Not a burden we bear, not a sorrow we share,
but our toil he doth richly repay.
Not a grief nor a loss, not a frown nor a cross,
but is bless'd if we trust and obey.

3. But we never can prove the delights of his love,
until all on the altar we lay,
for the favor he shows, and the joy he bestows,
are for them who will trust and obey.

4. Then in fellowship sweet we will sit at his feet,
or we'll walk by his side in the way.
What he says we will do, where he sends we will
   go,
never fear, only trust and obey.

John H. Sammis, 1887

3. Prosperity: "When we are faithful God rewards us materially." This ancient point of view can be traced to the patriarchs whose lives are recorded in the Hebrew Scripture. God's promise to bless Abraham so that he could be a blessing is carried over to what God wants to do for the Christian. A related chorus: "He owns the cattle on a thousand hills."

> He owns the cattle on a thousand hills
> The wealth in every mine.
> He owns the rivers and the rocks and rills
> The sun and the stars that shine
> Wonderful the riches more than tongue can tell
> He is my Father so they're mine as well.
> He owns the cattle on a thousand hills
> And I know that he will care for me.

Perception

Faith is connected to perception, the way we see life, the way we understand God. Through music, drama, poetry, dance, and the visual arts, the church shapes how people see God and the world. From this perception identity is shaped. Identity in turn dictates belief and behavior.

Perception is critical to how we talk with each other about money. Because people have different perceptions of God, and different perceptions of money, they will likely interpret the same Scripture text very differently. Those who come from a "wealthy heir" perspective (see chart "Speaking About Money" above) will see it completely different from those who perceive themselves as one of the "blessed poor."

my experience

	poverty	wealth
abundance	1. Impoverished Hopefuls	3. Wealthy Heirs
austerity	2. Blessed Poor	4. Freely Givers

my beliefs (left axis label spanning abundance/austerity)

Definitions

You will need the following definitions to help you understand the above diagram that describes the way our perceptions of experience and beliefs mix and mingle.

Perceptions based on experience

> **Poverty:** I am dependent on the work of the extended family and community in order to achieve life's basic needs.

> **Wealth:** I am independent of extended family and community in order to achieve life's basic needs, often with much left over.

Perceptions based on beliefs/values

> **Abundance:** "I give in faith that God will bless me. Or, I give trusting that God will provide. Or (in its most extreme form), "I give expecting God to give back to me."
>
> **Austerity:** "I give everything because Jesus gave everything." It doesn't mean you don't trust, but the root motivation is to follow the example of Jesus. Extreme manifestation: "It's my duty to give away my money because I'm supposed to."

With these definitions well in mind, study the chart. Note that the axis lines, vertical and horizontal, describe both experiences and beliefs. Ask yourself, *On the whole, which box best characterizes my life? On the whole, which box best characterizes my beliefs/values?* Be aware, each quadrant/perspective in itself is incomplete. Imagine yourself in the other quadrants, and you will start to sense how money is impacting your congregation. In most congregations there are representatives of all four experience/perception combinations. One quadrant is likely to be the dominant perspective, but not the only one, and maybe not the majority one!

Wholeness is found in expressing both the **inviting** and **excluding** of each quadrant edges (described on the following pages). Together the statements are true. By themselves, they are not enough.

"When that old stock market crashed, the next thing you knew, the world was falling apart. The newspapers were full of stories of rich white men who had committed suicide, jumping out of buildings, things like that. I can't imagine having so little faith in the Lord, and so much faith in money, that you would end your life over a little thing like losing your fortune. The Lord says money is Evil, and he is right! Money is the root of every mess you can think of, including slavery. Greed! Profiting off the backs of others!"

Having Our Say, The Delany Sisters' First 100 Years. Sarah L. Delany and A. Elizabeth Delany with Amy Hill Hearth, 1994, Bantam Doubleday Dell Publishing Group

Sometimes life experience changes in terms of money (we increase our wealth, we lose our wealth), and that causes a discordant note with where we have placed ourselves. It can help to tell and hear stories about how you grew up and the perspective you had. How has your perspective changed?

Description and use of diagram

See which of these descriptions seem to fit your life experience and beliefs/values.

Box 1: The impoverished hopeful

Perceptions held may include:

- I have a mix of poverty experiences and abundance beliefs.
- I give in faith that God will bless me, and I live dependent on family and community to meet life's basic needs.
- Poverty is not structural or systemic. You can pull yourself up by your bootstraps if you have enough hope and work hard enough.
- It is always a struggle to make ends met, but I find ways to be loving about life anyway.
- I look forward to heaven as the relief of my suffering.
- Definitive hymn, "On Jordan's Stormy Banks I Stand."

Refrain

I'm bound for the promised land, I'm bound for the promised land.

Oh, who will come and go with me? I'm bound for the promised land.

Verses

1. On Jordan's stormy banks I stand, and cast a
   wishful eye
to Canaan's fair and happy land, where my
   possessions lie.

2. There gen'rous fruits that never fail, on trees
   immortal grow.
There rocks and hills and brooks and vales with
   milk and honey flow.

3. All o'er those wide extended plains shines one
   eternal day.
There God the sun forever reigns, and scatters
   night away.

4. When shall I reach that happy place, and be for
   ever bless'd?
When shall I see my Father's face, and in his
   bosom rest?

5. Filled with delight, my raptured soul can here
   no longer stay.
Though Jordan's waves around me roll, fearless I'd
   launch away.

Samuel Stennett, 1787

Inviting edge

Revelation 21. A vision of the golden streets, hope,
something inviting beyond this world. God will take care
of you, you are a guaranteed lottery winner in the next
life, and can trust God to reward you with plenty. But if
you play the lottery in this life, you are not trusting God
for what you need!

Excluding edge

Job 8:1-8. The idle are punished, and if you feel help-
less you must have sinned. You will lose your reward if

you don't believe this way. If you are pure and upright, God rouses for you. Suffering is a result of sin, or a test. Life is a simple choice, either/or. Don't make looking for God's justice too complex.

Box 2: The blessed poor

Perceptions they might hold:

- I have a mix of poverty experiences and austerity beliefs.
- I give everything because Jesus gave everything, and live dependent on family and community to meet life's basic needs.
- I walk away from or shun riches because Jesus did.
- St. Francis, Mother Teresa, Dorothy Day, Bishop Oscar Romero, and the dignified poor are my heroes.
- Base communities of Central and South America are the ideal way to do church.
- Poverty is systemic, and God will rectify it.
- Definitive hymn "Take My Life."

Verses

1. Take my life, and let it be consecrated,
Lord, to thee. Take my moments and my days;
let them flow in ceaseless praise,
let them flow in ceaseless praise.

2. Take my hands, and let them move
at the impulse of thy love.
Take my feet, and let them be
swift and beautiful for thee,
swift and beautiful for thee.

3. Take my voice, and let me sing,
always, only for my King.

Take my lips, and let them be
filled with messages from thee,
filled with messages from thee.

4. Take my silver and my gold;
not a mite would I withhold.
Take my intellect and use
ev'ry pow'r as thou shalt choose,
ev'ry pow'r as thou shalt choose.

5. Take my will, and make it thine;
it shall be no longer mine.
Take my heart, it is thine own,
it shall be thy royal throne,
it shall be thy royal throne.

6. Take my love; my Lord, I pour
at thy feet its treasure store.
Take myself, and I will be
ever, only, all for thee,
ever, only, all for thee.

Frances R. Havergal, 1874

Inviting edge

Luke 6:20. Blessed are the poor. This "blessed" statement is about economics, not only about spiritual poverty. When you don't have, you more readily turn to God.
This means God loves the poor more than the rich, so we
who are poor might make it through this world without
experiencing God's judgment. Scripture's Advent songs
hold forth much of this perspective. Read the songs and
you find this reoccurring sentiment: the poor aren't
going to be poor anymore—things will be equalized!

Excluding edge

James 5:1-6. Woe to the rich! You are doomed! Depending on your position in life, some will hear this as an indictment, and others as a promise. A person of wealth will experience this as excluding, while the poor hear it as hope and salvation.

Box 3: The wealthy heir

Perceptions they might hold:

- I have a mix of wealth experiences and abundance beliefs.
- I should pay my own way, be a responsible person.
- I give in faith that God will bless me, and I live independent of family and community in meeting life's basic needs.
- God owns it all, and I get to help God manage it.
- If you don't have a material blessing, you don't have enough faith.
- If you're thrifty, take risks for God, and invest well, you will prosper.
- Poverty and wealth are not systemic. Anyone can rise above it.
- Self-determination and personal effort make the difference in one's economic status.
- Definitive hymn, "Jesus Is All the World to Me."

Verses

1. Jesus is all the world to me,
My life, my joy, my all;
He is my strength from day to day,
Without him I would fall.
When I am sad to him I go,
No other one can cheer me so;
When I am sad he makes me glad,
He's my friend.

2. Jesus is all the world to me,
My friend in trials sore;
I go to him for blessings,
And he gives them o'er and o'er.
He sends the sunshine and the rain,
He sends the harvest's golden grain;
Sunshine and rain, harvest of grain,
He's my friend.

3. Jesus is all the world to me,
And true to him I'll be;
O how could I this Friend deny,
When he's so true to me?
Following him I know I'm right,
He watches o'er me day and night;
Following him by day and night,
He's my friend.

4. Jesus is all the world to me,
I want no better friend;
I trust him now, I'll trust him when
Life's fleeting days shall end.
Beautiful life with such a Friend;
Beautiful life that has no end;
Eternal life, eternal joy,
He's my friend.

Will L. Thompson

Inviting edge

Deuteronomy 28:1-14. God's makes a covenantal promise of plenty to the faithful. God says he will bless you so that you can be a blessing. The danger with this inviting edge is the possible correlation between faithfulness and reward. It can lead to an "investment" relationship with God, a works doctrine that compels a believer to require God to respond, rather than bless people gratefully by grace.

Excluding edge

Luke 19:11-27. Parable of the pounds. The servant who does not put God-given endowments to work experiences eternal suffering and separation from God. If you aren't productive, you can expect drastic punishment. No quarter is given those who are victim to societal sin.

Box 4: The freely giver

Perceptions they might hold:

- I have a mix of wealth experiences and austerity beliefs.
- I give everything because Jesus gave everything, and do (or could) live independent of family and community to meets life's basic needs.
- I find freedom and joy when I give away, and so does anyone else.
- To love God means not loving money.
- Definitive hymn "Freely, Freely."

Verse

He forgave my sins in Jesus' name
I am born again in Jesus' name

Chorus

1. Freely, freely
You have received
Freely, freely
Give.
Go in my name
And because you believe
Others will know that I live.

Inviting edge

Luke 19:1-10. Zacchaeus, upon encountering Christ, immediately understands that his economic life is involved. "I'll give half my possessions to the poor. If I defrauded anyone, I will repay four times as much." Here is newfound freedom in generosity, no hesitation, as opposed to the rich young ruler who went away sad because of his attachment to his many possessions.

Excluding edge

Acts 5:1-11. Ananias and Sapphira. Yes, their great sin was not that they did not give everything, but that they lied to God. Had they given everything there would have been no lie. However, the implication is that if you are not free with your gift, you experience less of God's grace.

One Text: Four Perspectives

Life would be easier if any of the four perspectives were this simple. But it does not work that way. Those who hold to these perspectives can look at the same Scripture and interpret it for their advantage. Here is an example of how each perspective can work with one biblical story. The text is the story of Noah's sacrifice in Genesis 8 and 9.

Descending from the ark Noah didn't have much. Yet, as a first act of worship for the protection he and his family received, Noah made a burnt offering of the scarce animals in his possession. He declared his trust that God would continue to provide. The story tells us God smelled this sacrifice, and was so moved by Noah's ability to rise above selfishness that the Creator promised not to destroy the earth again—no matter the sin that humans might commit. It is a wondrous thing to know that God interacts with us in our giving. It brings divine action into the world. It affects the course of history. It moves and shakes the heavens. It puts rainbows in the sky.

People hear this story from each section of the grid, depending on their mix of experience and belief. Biblically all are valid and need not be in tension with each other. We reach the fullest understanding of the text by embracing all of them rather than choosing one against the others.

Impoverished hopeful—Noah gave anyway, even though he didn't have much. He trusted God to make up the difference.

Blessed poor—Noah could give to God without need of official religious institutions. Worship and religious life can happen at the level of this small clan that is working together to survive.

Wealthy heirs—The whole world belonged to Noah for his work and control. God blessed Noah and his family further as he honored him, taking care of creation as he did so.

Freely giver—Noah's act was given in the spirit of the way God gives to us. It was worship that altered history.

PART III

Talking about money in the church

Imagine asking these two questions in church:
First, how much money did you make last year?
Second, how did you spend it?

Taboo, right? But staying silent about how money affects us gives money a power it doesn't deserve, a power that competes with God. If you are a church leader, how do you break through the taboos, the silence? How do you conduct active listening about money matters? How is your perception about money expressed? How do you work through the money agenda in your life so that you can minister to others?

How can we offer all that we are and have in ways that are life giving? How can leaders help the congregation *rediscover* the true God, the God that is not money? Preaching is just one task. Leaders have to pay attention to two streams in the congregation's life:

1. Talking about money (How do we do it?)
2. Managing money (It IS the church's business!)

CHAPTER 5

The leader's role

"**P**astors just don't understand management and finance." A century ago most ministers supported themselves financially. If a minister could do that successfully, his or her word in congregational money matters carried weight. Today, pastoral responsibility may *itself* be the way a person earns a living. A pastor may not have had regular or serious business experience. Some pastors may have different priorities concerning money than church members do. Pastors may have trained themselves not to buy into the prevailing culture's mania and assumptions around money, and they may appear naive about money matters.

It's good for pastors to enjoy the assistance of others when working with financial and managerial matters. The apostles even created the office of deacon to help manage money so that the spiritual leadership could focus on biblical teaching and prayer. But too many pastors feel inadequate to manage their own finances, let alone provide spiritual instruction about money to anyone else. While they may benefit from the expertise of others, they *may also be vulnerable* to the ignorance of others.

Pastors have a fourfold challenge.
1. They must be exemplary money managers.
2. They must reflect the great generosity of God in the way they manage resources.

3. They need to be able to lead the church through intricate money decisions.
4. Pastors must understand the profound connection between spirituality and the use of money.

Money 101 for church leaders

Pastors are anxious when it comes to preaching on the subject of money. Usually they are afraid of sounding irrelevant, offending, or projecting the sense that money should be kept separate from spirituality.

But money questions in the congregation must be addressed by the spiritual leadership, simply because money is such a powerful force. Business, money, and theology are not antithetical topics of conversation. Don't be silent!

Pastors, elders, deacons, and other church leaders need to tell their life stories around money. Once church leaders renew themselves around personal issues of money, they will find courage and skill to improve their preaching and teaching about money.

Why? Consider this:

- Spending more than one earns and financing this excessive consumption with credit cards has become a habit for many church members.
- Money is the chief reason marriages fail.
- The number of people in congregations who run home-based or small businesses is up.
- There is a growing gap between the wealthiest and the poorest in North American society.
- People no longer expect to work at one job their entire lives.
- There is an increasing amount of economic anxiety in congregations, whether the economy is strong and wages are greater or whether the econ-

omy is shrinking and income disappears. Economic movement in any direction brings anxiousness.

- Baby boomers are finally beginning to save for retirement. They seem to be saving with the same all-out style with which they approached other stages of life.
- Young people are consistently quizzed on the career they think they will choose; followed by comments on how much money such a career choice can earn for them.
- Young adults are afraid they must bear the burden of environmental cleanup, along with funding social assistance for an ever-growing population of elderly people.
- Trillions of dollars are changing hands through inheritance. The amount is unprecedented.
- Churches carry greater debt loads than ever before because their members do the same. Churches give less money away because the people who attend them give less money away.
- More people must face the costs of a catastrophic health crisis without the benefit of insurance.
- The morality of fair play is breaking down, and it causes numerous ethical dilemmas for believers when they participate in the economy.
- Individual habits are expressed corporately. What congregational members do in their homes eventually becomes the precedent for what they decide to do together in the congregation.

Speaking about one's money life as an application of spirituality gives preachers greater impact on how the congregation and its members handle money. When you preach, address the spiritual lives of the congregation. With the preceding list of reasons for improving teaching and preaching, there is plenty of material, and there are plenty of angles.

The most effective leaders train themselves to be:

1. *Secure in God's merciful treatment of them.* Pastors, elders, deacons, and other church leaders aren't immune to struggling with money questions. In your plan for congregational renewal, don't skip the step of offering church leaders healing, hope, and accountability when anger, fear, pain, and sin come to the surface. Money autobiography events are a wonderful tool for this.

Once church leaders are renewed, they can lead members in a similar experience so that the congregation faces its relationship with money and takes new steps in discipleship and maturity.

2. *Aware of the dynamics of change* (see chapter 10). When a change is in the wind, every congregation discovers it has innovators, early adopters, middle adopters, late adopters, and never adopters. Leaders do well to learn what to expect from each of these groups. They also become adept at managing conversations aimed toward change.

3. *Nonanxious.* They are not readily affected by the anxiety of others. Leaders keep in mind the long view and the overarching goals of the congregation. They are gentle with people yet firm on agreed-to process.

4. *Patient.* Leaders are unhurried, committed to give people the necessary amount of time to develop ownership.

5. *Mission-oriented.* Leaders help people toward the chief end of ministry: **an ever-deepening and loving relationship with God.** Leaders keep in mind that this is more important than uniform perspective on economic issues!

6. Clear that agreement on *issues and process must be a first priority.* Working to agree on solutions cannot happen effectively without explicit agreement on what issues are being addressed, and what process will be followed in making decisions. This must be done before presenting any proposal.

Money 101 for congregations

While the church leadership is renewing itself around money issues, the congregation can do its part. It can

- Expect leadership development programs to prepare leaders to be wise managers of financial and human resources.

- Stop making the pastor's salary an annual point of contention in budget discussions. Instead, set a policy on the percentage of income you are willing to make available for staffing and allow the governing board to set the salaries within the available amount.

- Study the priorities for money collected by God's people (see sidebar).

- Develop and celebrate a reputation of generosity to their ministry staff.

Tithes collected by the Old Testament community went for three activities: (1) Firstfruits celebrations—a ceremonial recognition that God owned the land, and a celebration of God's provision; (2) the adequate provision for those ministering before the Lord; and (3) distribution to the needy. The New Testament confirms that this practice was continued in the early church. (See *A Christian View of Money: Celebrating God's Generosity,* chapter 7, for a fuller consideration of this matter.)

- Become deeply concerned that their money decisions reflect their corporate spirituality.

- Denominations can join the renewal by providing adequate support systems for pastors or congregations that are trying to break out of tired patterns, as well as model faithful and mature management practices. Then leaders will be more ready to lead.

Lead what?

Some faith communities are accustomed to their leadership determining what the church needs to do, then asking the church to fund it. But the opposite needs to happen. Leadership teaches that the most important thing is not program, but the **worshipful generosity of God's people**. Leaders give up control over the amount God's people give, and where it goes, and invites God's Spirit to set the pace.

Renew your connection between spirituality and money. Then renew the connection between your preaching and money. Finally renew your congregation around its spiritual life and money.

CHAPTER 6

Worship and money

Start with stressing firstfruits living—not leftover giving. This first major attitude change comes about through worship. The journey into firstfruits living is first and foremost an experience in receiving the grace of God. The sample worship services at the end of this chapter pages 78-87, highlight *experience, story, and practice,* a theme that arises from Deuteronomy 6:20-25. Notice how the *story* of the *experience* of receiving God's grace prompts *practice.*

The experience, story, and practice trilogy

Experience

When you hear the word "experience" in worship, you may think of the experience in giving. Think instead of experiencing God's grace in *receiving*. We become Christians by admitting our need for God's grace—receiving. God's kingdom is something we receive. It is in receiv-

When your children ask you in time to come, "What is the meaning of the decrees and the statutes and the ordinances that the Lord our God has commanded you?" then you shall say to your children, "We were Pharaoh's slaves in Egypt, but the Lord brought us out of Egypt with a mighty hand. The Lord displayed before our eyes great and awesome signs and wonders against Egypt, against Pharaoh and all his entire household. He brought us out from there in order to bring us in, to give us the land that he promised on oath to our ancestors. Then the Lord commanded us to observe all these statutes, to fear the Lord our God, for our lasting good, so as to keep us alive, as is now the case. If we diligently observe this entire commandment before the Lord our God, as he has commanded us, we will be in the right."
(Deuteronomy 6:20-25)

ing this grace that we find grace to give to others. Think of how the Exodus story overflows with God's gracious and generous care. The plagues, the Red Sea rescue, and the feeding in the desert are permanent reminders of a generous God. Those who are in touch with God as a sustaining source of grace are better equipped to live a generous life.

Story

Tell stories—give testimony—of meeting God's grace and how we responded with our own generosity. Tell both personal and family stories as well as congregational stories.

Storytelling should describe both the grace we receive and the giving we do. Our stories can tell about what happens when we hoard (Achan in Joshua 7), and when we are generous (offering for the tabernacle in Exodus 35:20ff.). The Exodus story is repeated in the Pentateuch, the Psalms, and in sermons by the prophets to remind people of God's grace.

Telling the story of receiving God's grace makes us conscious of our experience and reminds others of their experience. It invites believers to step into new faith ventures where they must once again live by the grace of God. Most importantly, storytelling invites people to respond to God's grace when they have never known it or have lost touch with it.

Practice

There are two ways we follow through on our experience with God's grace:

- First, practice in giving through acts of worship and hospitality.
- Second, practice in deciding on the distribution of funds collected in worship.

The Hebrew people offered burnt offerings (Leviticus 1), knowing the entire gift would be consumed in worship to God. They also consecrated other gifts and sacrifices to God's use. Finally, they were involved in the distribution. For instance, they knew their gifts would be used to construct the tabernacle (Exodus 35). They knew a portion of their grain offering would be given to priests and their families (Leviticus 2). They knew their firstfruits gifts would be partly offering in worship, partly used for a community feast at God's house, and partly given to others for their use (Deuteronomy 14).

They also had clear instruction on the practice of hospitality such as caring for the widow, the orphan, their faith community, even the stranger and the alien. Hospitality, a moral imperative, included leaving generous "gleanings" in their fields, and refraining from shady business practices.

Experience, stories, and practice are all part of firstfruits living. If you experience God's grace, you will have a story to tell, and you will act in a different way. Therefore, let us:

- Foster interdependence rather than independence. Teach and encourage an ability to receive, so that the ability to give may follow.
- Break the silence by telling stories about our life with money. Not letting the "left hand know what the right hand is doing" (Matthew 6:3) is an instruction concerning almsgiving. It is not intended to silence our public declaration of God's sovereignty over our money.
- Practice the joy of collecting and distributing funds for ministry. Solicit the ideas of all participants, not just an elite and older cadre of longtime attendees. Boldly step forward with new faith prac-

tices that foster an increasing reliance on the grace of God.

More money applications, not more stewardship sermons

Money, materialism, and consumption have godlike powers. Nothing else competes for our attention and threatens with such intensity to unseat God. Therefore, a pastor's preaching and teaching about money must be just as powerful. Such power comes from personal renewal.

If you want to strengthen your preaching about money, address your fear. Many pastors are so nervous about texts that tackle money that they apologize: *"If you're visiting with us today, understand that I only preach on stewardship once a year."* [1] They worry about offending the wealthy, showing their ignorance about economics, failing to understand the difficulty of being poor, or becoming the victim of congregational anger.

Pastor Robert Russell admits that his fear of talking about money came from cowardice. "The reason I wasn't preaching on stewardship was [because] I wanted to please people more than I wanted to please God." [2] As he faced those fears, Russell ultimately discovered "people really do want to hear what the Bible says about money, because it's a matter close to the heart and such a divisive issue for families." [3]

Facing these fears does not happen by preaching more stewardship sermons. What the congregation really needs is spiritual renewal around the issue of money. Instead of more stewardship sermons, effective preaching must address the subject of money consistently and systematically. Concerns about money break up marriages, tempt people to abandon their moral codes, and lead people into elaborate webs of self-deception. The use and abuse of money dominates the spiritual agenda of Christians. Don't avoid the subject!

Include in your preaching more recognition of how money competes with God in the marketplace and family. Talking about money and its uses connects Sunday faith to life outside the church walls.

Six questions to ask in sermon preparation

How should one preach with more money applications? Because money is such a pervasive part of life, when life and faith intersect, there is usually a money application.

First, start with how a sermon is put together:

Exegesis is the effort to understand the biblical text. Preachers or teachers who do their job well struggle to answer these two questions:[4]

1. What is the biblical writer talking about?
2. What is the biblical writer saying about it?

When you have boiled down answers to these questions with a tightly worded sentence, you can be confident that you have captured the essence of the text. But it isn't a sermon yet.

The second stage of sermon preparation is called the *exegesis of the audience.* Without understanding the audience a leader can hardly hope to effectively communicate the subject. So answer these two questions:

1. Who will be in the audience? Does anyone connect to the text in a unique way?
2. How can I communicate God's message in a way they will be able to hear it?

The third stage is *homiletics,* figuring out how to get the message across. Answer these two questions:

1. Based upon my understanding of the text and the audience, what will I talk about?
2. What will I say about it?

When you've answered these in a tightly worded sentence, you have a nugget of truth to communicate in sermonic form.

Six questions to ask in sermon preparation

Exegesis of text
1. What is the biblical writer talking about?

Answer:

2. What is the biblical writer saying about it?

Answer:

Exegesis of audience

3. Who will be in the audience? Does anyone connect to the text in a unique way?

Answer:

4. How can I communicate God's message in a way they will be able to hear it?

Answer:

Homiletics

5. Based upon my understanding of the text and audience, what is God saying to us?

Answer:

6. What would God have me say about it?

Answer:

Here is an example using Acts 4:32—5:11 as the sermon text. The story is about the generosity of Barnabas and the deception of Ananias and Sapphira.

1. In answering the *exegetical* questions I settle on the sentence: "As the early church dealt with money and possessions, some were motivated by a profound level of grace, while others were motivated by selfishness and a desire for recognition."
2. In *exegeting the audience,* I note that my congregation has a number of business owners, one family of recent immigrants from Asia, three families experiencing unemployment, a dozen teenagers who are working at their first jobs, and fifteen

retired couples. The congregation is largely lower middle-class. Many feel their purchasing power and economic lifestyles are declining. Hitting them over the head with a sermon on Ananias and Sapphira's deception might produce even more economic despair, and failure to be open to God's word. Throughout my preparations I ask how business owners will hear the Scripture and my comments, how those from different ethnic groups will hear this sermon, what might get a teen's attention, and how those who have much to give and those in great need will react to what they hear.

3. So after exegeting my audience and working with the *homiletic* questions, I choose Acts 4:33 as the key verse and decide to preach on the stream of grace—how Christians who drink deeply of this stream find that it flows through them to others.

I decide to call three to five lay people known for their generosity. I share with them the plans for my sermon, and ask them to share one or two practical ways they demonstrate God's grace to others. These testimonies become the sermon's application. Their sharing becomes a realistic way of applying the text to life.[5]

Cautions

Watch out! Because of your own money perception, you might have another interpretation of these texts. You might also avoid certain texts, miss their economic message, or resent what someone else draws from them. Be continually aware that you have a mixture of Impoverished Hopefuls, Blessed Poor, Wealthy Heirs, and Freely Givers in your church (see chapter 4). One quadrant is likely the dominant perspective in a congregation, but not the only perspective, and maybe not even the majority one. Wholeness is found in expressing the inviting and excluding edges of each quadrant: together they are true; by themselves they are not enough.

You are likely to find one or more of these *inviting* messages about money (even indirectly) in most passages of Scripture:
- We have a hope in God's abundance.
- God cares about the poor.
- We are part of God's family and enjoy the benefits.
- We can know the joy of freedom from concern about money.

You are also likely to be able to identify one of these *excluding* messages about money, possibly in the same passage:
- Sin produces punishing results, often economic.
- Trusting in riches is a curse.
- Not investing in God's concerns brings separation from God.
- Slavery to money is death.

Both the excluding and the inviting messages need to be preached in order for the whole of the biblical message to be heard. These messages are not a menu from which you choose. Each theme needs to be addressed.

Exercise
1. Choose one of these biblical passages.
   Joshua 23
   Psalm 61
   Mark 10:13-16
   Ephesians 4:25-32
   Revelation 1:4-7

2. Use the worksheet, "Six Questions to ask in Sermon Preparation," which follows to:
- Answer the exegetical and homiletical questions.
- Include a money or economic application not related to giving. Remember, applications include *what you want people to know, what people are to believe, what people will try, what people will do.*

Six questions to ask in sermon preparation

Exegesis of text

1. What is the biblical writer talking about?
Answer:
2. What is the biblical writer saying about it?
Answer:

Exegesis of audience

3. Who will be in the audience? Does anyone connect to the text in a unique way?
Answer:

4. How can I communicate God's message in a way they will be able to hear it?
Answer:

Homiletics

5. Based upon my understanding of the text and audience, what is God saying to us?
Answer:

6. What would God have me say about it?
Answer:

Sample worship service outlines from Giving Project Gatherings

Worship A (Experience)

Purpose

To convey that the journey into stewardship is first and foremost an experience in receiving the grace of God.

Call to worship (Deuteronomy 6:20-25)
Hymn (processional, include elements for communion)
Welcome
Prayer
Two hymns
Confession
Scripture reading—Psalm 105:1-6
Sermon
Communion (invite the congregation to come forward to receive the elements; provide a moist/perfumed towel for washing hands as people move to the side aisles and to their seats)
Hymn of response
Prayer and passing of the peace

Worship B (Story)

Purpose

To remind us of the grace we have received, and to provide a venue for sharing stories of grace.

Gathering hymns (3-5)
Call to worship (Deuteronomy 6:20-25)
Welcome
Hymns
Story of grace
Response chorus ("Grace, grace, God's grace, grace that will pardon and cleanse within. . . .")

Story of grace
Response chorus

Story of grace
Response chorus

Scripture reading—Psalm 105:7-42
Speaker
Response hymn
Closing prayer

Worship C (practice)

Purpose

To call attention to the responses we can make as recipients of God's grace.

Gathering hymns (3-5)
Call to worship (Deuteronomy 6:20-25)
Welcome

Response 1: monetary offering (congregation comes forward)
Two praise and worship hymns

Response 2: praise offering (congregation is asked to offer names and descriptions of God while music continues)
One praise/worship hymn

Response 3: prayer for each other (congregation is invited to share with a partner in triad regarding God's call, then pray for one another)
Hymn (theme hymn calls everyone back to their seats)

Scripture—Psalm 105:43-45
Speaker
Response hymn
Closing prayer

Worship D: Experience/story/practice as a whole

Purpose

To give God an extended offering.

Gathering hymns (3-5)
Call to worship (Deuteronomy 6:20-25)
Welcome

Experience

Psalm 105:1-6
Comments
Offering of symbols (congregation is invited to bring
  something that symbolizes the grace of God in
  their life)

Story

Psalm 105: 7-42
Comments
Offering of stores (congregation is invited to tell
  brief stories of grace about which they can no
  longer remain silent)
Hymn

Practice

Psalm 105:43-45
Comments
Offering of practice (congregation is invited to share
  faith practices that they intend to begin)
Hymn
Closing prayers and sending

Meditations on Psalm 105

I. Experience (vv. 1-7). (May be used with services A and D.)

Psalm 105 lives in two dimensions:
- The "We"
- The "Me"
- Psalm 105 is both personal and corporate—we and me. Every phrase invites me and we into remembering our experience with God's grace, to tell the story of that grace yet again, and to listen to the invitation to practice obedience to what the Lord requires.
- For now, with these first seven verses of the psalm, we return to the beginning of our experience with grace, reminding ourselves of the meaning of experiencing God's interest in us, to know that God desires a relationship with us—in spite of our limitations, even though we sin. And how does the psalmist suggest we keep the experience in front of us? Listen to the commands:

* Give thanks to the Lord.
* Call on the Lord's name (given the context of praise, this is not calling out of intercession, but from exultation in what God has done).
* Make known God's deeds among the peoples.
* Sing to God—especially songs of praise.
* Speak of God's wonders.
* Glory in God's holy name.

  The word "glory" is worth dwelling on since so many of us struggle to express great joy in our religious life. In this psalm we have permission to luxuriate in God's work like we do when we sink into a hot bath after strenuous activity, or when we press a cool glass against our face on a hot summer day, or like the time Lorie and I caught our then two-year-old daughter quaffing a chocolate milk shake like a Norse god drinks mead. She clearly was enjoying the full body experience of streams of chocolate going down her throat and the sides of her face onto her white Sunday dress. Through laughter Lorie told her, "Honey that's not the way we drink a milk shake." Autumn replied, "But Mommy, that's the way I am!"

* Let your heart be glad—especially those who are seeking the Lord.

At the mention of seeking the Lord, it makes sense to move from exhortations to praise to invitations to reflect. And that is exactly what the psalmist does.

* Seek the Lord and his strength.
* Seek the Lord's face continually.
* Remember the wonders the Lord has done (and his marvels).
* Remember the judgments uttered by his mouth.

And now the psalmist shifts yet again to expand on the judgments uttered by God. Remember, the psalmist tells us, the God who utters these judgments is <u>our</u> God, is <u>my</u> God, and the judgments God utters are all around us. Our experience with God's grace makes us Abraham's seed, children of Jacob. We stand in the middle of God's family, accepted and loved.

Perhaps you have something with you that symbolizes God's grace in your life. For me it is the copper bracelet I wear on my wrist. Sometimes I hold it in my hand to help me concentrate on my praying. Always, it reminds me of the high desert, a special place for me in feeling peace and closeness to God. One time in particular, while driving across the Mojave late at night on a moonless and clear night, I had a wonderful view of the Hale Bopp comet. Out on that desolate landscape I was a couple of thousand feet higher, and the sky was clearer, and the dark was greater to set a contrast with the natural light that comes from the heavens. That night put me in awe of God in a deeper way. It is an appropriate act to bring a symbol like this to the altar as an act of offering our praise to God for the privilege of knowing his grace. After this worship service you will pick up these symbols again, but you will do so knowing these symbols are dedicated for God's continued flow of grace into your life, and that we need to remain in the posture of receiving that grace.

As we sing, come and offer your symbols of experiencing the grace of God.

II. Story (vv. 8-41). (May be used with services B and D.)

Have you ever noticed that when people begin telling their story of coming to faith, they often start with their parents' spirituality, or lack of it, before moving to themselves? We notice the same thing when people tell their money autobiographies. Within the first minute, they unconsciously begin referring to the values they saw in their parents, or even their grandparents.

> Whenever I am asked to tell my faith story, I can't help but trace it to my Grandpa Vincent. It just feels like the starting point—how God brought him and his siblings to Shipshewana to be raised by an aunt, how he became a Christian at Shore Mennonite Church, how he and my Grandma Grace raised their children to be people of faith, how my Grandmother labored in prayer over each new life

that came into the Vincent household—children as well as grandchildren—how through their influence and the influence of my parents I came into my own faith.

A similar reaching into history happens in this psalm. In fact, you could look at Psalm 105 as the *Reader's Digest* condensed version of the Old Testament. God made a people (experience). Here is how God made the people (story). And here is the right response for those who experience God's grace (practice).

This psalm moves from the covenant with Abraham, Isaac, and Jacob to the captivity and exodus. The promise was to give the land of Canaan as an inheritance, and the story is retold of how it came to be. The theme throughout is that God was in it all.

- God was in the covenantal promise.
- God was in Joseph's captivity and exaltation.
- God was in the timing of the famine that restored Joseph to his family, and brought that family to Egypt to grow in numbers.
- God was present in their being enslaved.
- God was the one who raised up Moses and Aaron.
- God was the agent behind the plagues that brought freedom.
- God was the rescuer that brought them out.
- God was in the miracle of receiving lavish gifts from those who once enslaved them.
- God was the protector in the wilderness wanderings.
- God was the provider of food and meat and water.

This is a baseline story, the story that forms an identity rooted in experiencing the grace of God.

Are you carrying a story of God's grace that needs to be told? Perhaps the story is connected to the symbol you offered earlier. Don't forget the commands of this psalm to make known the marvels that God has done. Bless God and enhance our understanding of God's grace by sharing those stories with us.

III. *Practice (vv. 42-45).* (May be used with Worship Services C and D.)

Experiencing God's grace calls for a response, a way of living that honors the Giver of grace. This psalm's last verses pick up the same refrain, and it does so by condensing the cycle of experience, story, and practice even further.

1. God made a holy promise to Abraham (experience).
2. God brought his people out of captivity with a joyful shout and into a harvest they didn't plant (story).
3. So they might keep God's statutes and give God praise (practice).

Notice that by the time the practice of obeying and praising is introduced, it is no longer a duty or an instruction, but an appropriate response to a loving God. In the case of the Hebrews their keeping God's law grew from the experience of God's grace in the exodus. In our situation, we follow after Jesus because his grace covers our sin and brings us into God's family.

The practice we take on is borne from identity—who I am and who WE are—instead of manipulation or pressure. An identity provides a longer and more consistent reason to participate in these practices. An identity even names the practices in which we will engage.

Look at verse 15. God says his children are anointed ones (people set apart to serve God/little Christ's) and are prophets (people who tell the truth of what God wants along with the consequences).

Since you are receivers of God's grace, you are anointed prophets too! You are people who serve Christ and tell the truth. What new practices does this text invite you to? Let's offer these to God as well.

Notes

1. Robert Russell, *Leadership*, "Taming My Fears: Why I No Longer Back Away from Preaching About Money," Spring 1996, p. 95.
2. Ibid., p. 95-96.
3. Ibid., p. 96.
4. I am grateful to Duane Litfin, current president of Wheaton College, for these ideas.
5. A worksheet for sermon preparation is one of the resources in this section of the guide. *See page 77.*

CHAPTER 7

Preparing the ground for talking about money

How do leaders help people rediscover the true God, the God that is not money? Chapters 7 and 8 offer some strategies.

Long-term training in firstfruits living

Firstfruits living means offering the first and best of our lives to God in worship and using the rest in generous ways that honor God. Congregations and individuals can unpack this definition by exploring these questions:

- What does it mean to "*offer*"?
- What is the "*first and best*"?
- What part of our "*lives*"?
- What does it mean to "*worship God*"?
- What is the "*rest*"?
- What are "*generous ways that honor God*"?

Firstfruits emphasize giving as worship. Firstfruits festivals in the Hebrew Bible were celebrations of worship to God.

- Firstfruits living is not rooted in law, yet it sets a clear direction.
- Firstfruits involves all of life, not just money, and not only what we give at church
- Firstfruits emphasize grace.

- Firstfruits remind us that God owns everything.
- Firstfruits living reminds us of the right reason for giving: not because we happen to be on a spiritual high, nor from duty or obligation, but because of our identity as *God's* firstfruits. We give because of whose we are, remembering God's firstfruits gift to us: Jesus.

Firstfruits *commitments* are an estimate of income and giving for a fiscal year. Participants write their estimates on a card as an act of their worship. Congregational leaders use the sum of these firstfruits commitments to aid in the creation of a spending plan for the upcoming year. Why? Giving the first and the best of our incomes declares our love for God. We do not put money in the offering plate to meet a budget. We do not give to keep the church doors open. We give as an act of worship. Bringing estimates invites people to understand giving as worship. Participants are invited to plan their firstfruits lifestyle. This is **a spiritual exercise beneficial to all that participate.** It is the most important reason for encouraging this practice. The second benefit, the ability to more accurately create a spending plan, is only icing on the cake.

Working with the treasurer to treat giving as a window to pastoral care issues

Can a congregation's leadership know the incomes and giving percentages of congregational members? Absolutely. It's time to end the debate.

There are at least three reasons for leaders to become acquainted with giving patterns of congregational members, and to make it part of their ongoing system of pastoral care.

    1. Secrecy adds power. Christians need a place to identify their money struggles, name their temptations, seek counsel, and find healing and hope. We give money additional power in our lives when we pretend it doesn't influence us, or when we pretend all is well when it's not.

2. **Use of money is a window to spirituality.** Church leaders should pay attention to giving patterns, because the use of money communicates one's spirituality. When someone reduces their giving to the congregation, there is a reason. Perhaps their spiritual disciplines are slipping. Maybe they feel isolated. Maybe there is an economic need the church can surround and help. When someone increases their giving, perhaps it is because they have come to a deeper level of spiritual commitment, experienced some economic abundance, or feel more deeply connected to congregational life. When someone increases or decreases their giving, the treasurer should notify the pastoral caregiver, who makes note of this spiritual indicator for the next pastoral call. The important question the caregiver asks has nothing to do with money. Rather it is a fundamental question of spiritual direction: *"How are things between you and God?"* This is all they need to ask.

3. **Pastors are entrusted with other matters of confidentiality.** Pastors must handle all kinds of difficult matters of confession and confidentiality. Certainly they are capable of being confidential about money. **If not, the issue runs far deeper than mere knowledge about someone's use of money.** Not betraying a trust is part of the pastoral task. Holding confidences about matters of money is no different from those private conversations connected to sex, violence, or any other past secret.

Some may argue that when a pastor knows someone's income and giving patterns, he or she may treat them differently. Probably so. That might not be all bad! If I knew someone was not worshiping God with the income put within their trust, I might not take them as seriously when they complain about budget increases. When I know someone is giving sacrificially out of a deep love for God and God's church, I am more likely to hear the weight of any concerns he or she expresses. The amount of money is not a factor. It is a question of involvement.

In the fast-growing Meserete Kristos Church (500 congregations in five years), most are poor—the average wage for a teacher is $100 a month. Here is their giving procedure: First, all members tithe. Congregations hold members to their promises to do this.

Second, Sunday morning offerings are given in addition to the tithes. Neither the tithes nor offerings are used for church construction. Building funds come from special fundraising efforts. They put other financial priorities ahead of church construction (from an editorial by Paul Schrag in the *Mennonite Weekly Review*, April 25, 1996).

So don't make church giving the *only* gauge of spiritual health or else it becomes monitoring. It's *not* for monitoring church income in order to meet the budget! It isn't concerned with amounts but with temperature fluctuations. Ask: *How are things for you? How is it with you and God?*

This is the first place to break down this wall of secrecy. Money shouldn't have the power to erect a barrier between you and another person.

Dedicating offerings

Is your offering a celebration or a funding mechanism?

In the Hebrew Bible, bringing firstfruits offerings was a central focus in the worship of Yahweh. In the book of Acts, sharing economic resources was part of the core identity of the Jerusalem church. Only a few contemporary North American churches have maintained these understandings. Perhaps we are uncertain what to do with the offering because we have divided hearts. It's tough to bring both of our gods into the same building on Sunday mornings!

Receiving an offering was, in ancient Israel, an integral part of worship, and it can be again a time for God's people to declare their sole allegiance to and sole dependence on their Maker. Receiving an offering is a weekly opportunity for expressing the "worth-ship" of God. Instead of despairing of what to "do" with the offering time, we need to claim the opportunity!

How to reclaim a sense of worship in offering

In his career as a firstfruits minister, Lynn Miller often conducts spontaneous offerings by inviting everyone to take money out of their wallets, making sure everyone next to them had something to give. He distributes money to people, who are unprepared, so everyone can participate. Next, Lynn invites everyone to exchange gifts with someone sitting near them. That way, the focus is on giving a love gift to God rather than on the amount of the gift. Then he invites everyone to come forward and put their gifts in an offering plate he holds at the front of the church, singing hymns of praise as they come.

Finally, Lynn lifts the plate heavenward and dedicates the gifts for God's purposes. The prayer is simple. He declares the congregation's love for God and their desire for the gifts to glorify God's reign.

Dedicating offerings is a simple procedure. Here are the five major components:
1. *Receive* offerings. Don't *take* them. Offering lets us acknowledge God as the owner of all. Use lan-

guage that reflects that perspective.

2. Even if you pray before the offering, always *offer a prayer of dedication* at the end so that the gifts are formally and publicly given to God. Although written prayers and litanies that involve the congregation can be used from time to time, the best prayers of dedication are heartfelt descriptions of how we expect the money will be used.

3. *Encourage weekly giving.* Those who get paid every two weeks, monthly, or quarterly can divide their checks accordingly, or give smaller amounts on the "off" weeks. Those who give through automatic withdrawal can give copies of their transactions. Those who come unprepared can be given money so they, too, can participate. The idea is for the entire congregation to participate.

4. *Make the offering double as stewardship education.* This need not take long. As the offering is introduced, received, or even as you pray, you can reinforce important beliefs about Christians and money.

5. *Use the offering as a time of congregational participation in the worship theme.* Worship leaders should plan the offering in a way that will reinforce the worship theme.

Encourage non-monetary giving, so that it becomes clearer that God is after people's lives, including money. We could also offer:

- words of encouragement to other church members
- garden produce
- get-well notes for a church member who just completed surgery
- statements of praise to God
- our repentance from sin

- pledges of time
- periods of fasting
- our lives (parent-child blessings, baptisms, anointings)
- estimates of giving from future income
- our personal needs
- our suffering
- material goods we wish to share with others or contribute to the congregation's ministry

Nurturing leadership

"*Forming* the character of stewards means *converting* them, because conversion is the same developmental process as formation," insisted John Westerhoff pointedly in an address at the 1999 North American Stewardship Conference in Toronto. He continued, "It comes from practicing Christianity as a way of life, from seeing others practice that way of living. Those who practice it, come to it."

How we transfer leadership between generations is critical to converting stewards. Leaders develop and prepare their replacements. If they don't, they are merely managers, protecting what exists, instead of launching into the future.

It's not easy. When someone has a long history with his or her dwelling, for example, it's often difficult for the owner to return once he or she sells it. Why? Because the new family places a distinct mark of ownership on the place, distinguishing the home from what it was. The former owner may even believe his or her tastes and preferences have been turned aside as worthless.

The same phenomenon happens in the church. When newcomers want to change service times, pew positions, church education patterns, and committee job descriptions, the church's comfortable traditions get tweaked. But churches are not monuments to those who built them. They exist to pass on historic truths to those who follow. Churches continue only as newcomers are allowed to feel at home. And "home" means they get to bring the "furniture" with them, and maybe even choose some new pieces as well.

Watch out for these signs belying a cycle of leadership *prevention*:

- "We've never done it that way before."
- "Those young folks will eventually grow up."
- "I'm against it."
- "I don't feel heard."
- "Why would you want to do it that way?"
- "I don't belong."
- "Those old-timers don't know anything."
- The established generation begins to hoard church resources, protect its work, tries to control, is afraid of how *its* church will be changed by younger and newer people.
- Newer generations begin to reject tradition, to grow resentment toward church leaders, and to form a notion of what the church should be based on, what they are *against* rather than on what God is *for.*

How to break the cycle

Begin with hospitality to newcomers in the church community. Extend it to developing leadership skills in youth. Each generation must take responsibility for its own actions, and refuse to play its traditional role in the destructive leadership prevention cycle.

In order to build up Christ's reign (rather than perpetuate our own), we have to focus on *doing* discipleship over *preserving* methods of getting it done. Change comes more easily when we remember that the divine reign we proclaim is *already established* in Christ. God isn't so much interested in how we make a difference in this world, but more in how we *live in the difference God has already made,* and not through the structures *we* create.

Four suggestions for leadership development between generations of Christians:

1. Hospitality

Hospitality is a generous dispensing of what one has rather than seeking to get more. A church that practices Christian beliefs about money will make it a priority to be a welcoming and hospitable community. Their homes and possessions are no longer retained for private use, but become continuing gifts to neighbors and church communities. Without hospitality, churches find it difficult to extend a convincing invitation for newcomers to share in expanding God's reign.

In the past, hospitality usually meant inviting someone home after church for a meal. Although some people might want to resurrect this enjoyable practice, it is not the only way. People practice hospitality whenever they invite others into a journey with generosity. It is the no-strings-attached way we develop relationships, express interest in the lives of others, and put down roots of trust that can later bloom into a desire to join or continue one's participation in the work of a Christian community.

2. Assimilation of new members

People need access to relationships if they ever hope to call a church home, or begin to contribute to God's work from the wealth they manage. Gratitude and responsibility are not inbred; they must be developed. The best sort of responsibility is one rooted in gratitude. It grows as one trusts the faith community and feels needed. New members are assimilated into the congregation when gratitude, trust, connection, and response are in proper place.

Gratitude means—I am peaceful with the knowledge that God accepts me, and thankful for the gifts I receive in Jesus Christ. I am pleased to find others who share these insights, and who, because they experience God's acceptance of them, reach out to accept me.

Trust means—learning to give and receive counsel, to care and be cared for. It is having confidence that leadership seeks to discern God's direction, and that my input is valued.

Connection means—having seven to twelve significant relationships with people in the congregation. It means I have help to identify my ministering gifts and am happy to put them to work. I am committed to mutual aid.

Response means—worshiping God along with my church family—with my presence, with my praise, and with my firstfruits lifestyle.

3. Leadership cultivation tools

Leadership development, especially among those not seeking formal ordination, is receiving new attention. A strong ministry of calling out gifts among its members strengthens a church's ministry by broadening its resource pool. It also increases people's investment in ministry, and can energize them for spreading out the mantle of ministry over as many believers as possible, including new generations. Consultants for The Giving Project are prepared to point congregations toward specific resources for cultivating leadership.[1]

4. Youth groups and money

The average youth has a higher percentage of *discretionary* income than the average adult does. Youth are highly relational. They will not give to something unseen, unknown, or unfelt. Youth do not necessarily hope for a better world, or a brighter tomorrow. Joy that can be experienced now is more valuable than a joy that might not come later. Therefore, they do not always see the reason for a long-term commitment. Youth have also had to learn to cope with divorce and remarriage in their families, changes in gender roles, and rapid changes in other areas of life. These make them far more comfortable with standing between polarities rather than choosing between them.

One way to address these dynamics is to work with the youth group in managing its own money, just as the congregation does. (For a more comprehensive treatment on developing youth toward generosity within the congregation, see: Eugene C. Roehlkepartain, Elanah Dalyah Naftali and Laura Musegades, *Growing Up Generous: Engaging Youth in Giving and Serving*, The Alban Institute, 2000, 197 pp.)

What if a youth group, whether three or thirty in size, were challenged to begin to live a firstfruits lifestyle themselves, not just to support a financial plan determined by older adults? Here is one example:

A sixteen-year-old with an after-school job might have a financial worksheet that looks like this:

Hamburger Hut pays me	=	$ 6.50 an hour
I average	=	12 hours a week
I average	=	$ 156 per pay period
I expect to earn	=	$4,056 this year

Sallee Heinsbaugh is in her third year of serving as youth sponsor. The youth group is small—five females and three males. One will be a senior. Three out of the eight recently completed their freshman year. Last year these eight youth added up their expected incomes for the year:

Patsy	=	$450 (a combination of baby-sitting and allowance)
Jeremy	=	$500 (mowing lawn)
Heather	=	$1500 (cleaning her Dad's office three days a week)
Holly	=	$2000 (life guarding at the community pool)
Tim	=	$3500 (Cheeseburger Paradise)
Kerrie	=	$3600 (secretarial help at a law office)
Simon	=	$3800 (a little bit of everything)
Sarah	=	$4300 (veterinary clinic)

Then they covenanted together to contribute 10 percent of their incomes to the youth program for the year. This totaled a giving estimate of $1,965. Then, as a group, they met with the church council.

"We figure it will cost us $6,500 to attend two youth events, and to participate in next summer's denominational youth convention," they said. "Last year we raised almost that amount with three car washes, auctioning off the pastor's beard, our annual dinner theater, a stuffed-animal sale, and ten different bake sales after church events. We'd like to try it differently this next year. We are committing $2,000 of our own earnings toward the youth program. We would like the church to match it two for one, with the hope that our activities can be geared more toward service and ministry than fundraising. We'd still like to do the annual dinner theater event, since it goes over so well. This would give us a small financial cushion for the next year."

See *Teaching a Christian View of Money* for more ideas for nurturing leadership and making connections between givers and receivers.

Note

1. Contact MMA's Stewardship Education Center, 800-348-7468 or stewardship@mma-online.org.

CHAPTER 8

Leading people through money decisions

Narrative spending plans and reporting

Most churches establish some form of a budget, then hope the money comes in through a weekly offering and through member pledges. When we succeed in "meeting a budget," we tend to think *we* hit it, rather than continue a celebration of God's generosity.

Starting with a budget, then, doesn't enable a congregation to manage its finances according to God's values, or to do effective stewardship education. Here is why: If we believe that giving the first and best of our incomes is one way to declare our love for God, then we demonstrate this perspective by giving and distributing funds as an act of worship in a Christian community. The premise of giving and distribution cannot be the preservation of an institution. The basis must be worship.

A church that practices firstfruits giving develops individuals who practice firstfruits giving. Churches that wait until all local bills are covered before it contributes to God's work beyond themselves teach church members to do the same with their income.

An alternative to a budget is a **narrative-spending plan**. This is the *story* of what a congregation expects to do in the giving year. A church might use its mission statement to describe what it will do:

1. Proclaim the reign of God in worship.
2. Proclaim the reign of God through ministry.
3. Proclaim the reign of God through community life.

In writing a narrative-spending plan, a financial story for the upcoming year, the congregation estimates the costs of accomplishing their goals, and the spending of money to make them happen. This spending plan bases financial management on distributing funds for ministry, rather than the need to get ever more money from the congregation. It focuses on *doing* rather than *maintaining*. It connects people to the mission.

With such a plan in place, the congregation no longer needs a line item budget, only a chart of accounts. A line item budget only tells the congregation the amount of money appropriated and dispersed by various committees and programs of the church. A narrative-spending plan tells the congregation about the intended results. Narrative spending plans outline distributions of a congregation on a weekly basis, rather than only during the annual budget process. (For more examples of narrative spending plans, see *Teaching a Christian View of Money*, by Mark Vincent, 1997, Scottdale, Pa.: Herald Press).

Building projects

Planning any major construction initiative is ticklish business. Do too little and people refuse to discuss it until more detail is available. Do too much and it feels as if rubber stamps are expected. Leading a major monetary initiative means balancing planning and listening—listening and planning—always ready to revise or explain the reasons why. If the process is poorly led, money dynamics will add intensity to any disagreement on priorities.

These charts demonstrate how one church helped its members evaluate how their building project matched with the congregation's sense of mission.

Chart 1

Mission / Project Goals	Guided by God's call	Joyous sign of God's healing and hope: worshipful and joyous	Expresses faith and love through service in our community	Expresses faith through service at home	Expresses faith through service at work	Expresses faith through service in the world
Functional		*	*			
Accessible	*	*	*			
Globally sensitive	*	*				*
Spacious for growth	*	*	*			
Helpful for identity	*		*	*		*
On current site			*			
Toward future church planting	*	*	*			
Embraces change				*	*	
Builds up people	*	*	*	*		*

Chart 1, page 103

Notes for chart 1: Earlier congregational leaders were asked to identify the key goals the congregation would have for a successful building project. These goals are noted on the left-hand side. Leaders are asked to note their perception of how these goals intersect with the congregation's mission, which was broken down into column titles across the top (congregational members can also participate in this exercise).

Chart 1 reflects one person's perception. These perceptions are then tabulated to determine the weight of each goal in helping the congregation decide its project priorities.

Chart 2, page 105

Notes for chart 2: Assuming that chart 1 reflected the combined perception of the congregation, the goals are weighted as demonstrated across the top of chart 2.

In filling out chart 2, leaders and congregational members now give their perceptions of specific proposals for the facility. As they do, the appropriate numeric value is assigned to each. These values are totaled across the right. The facility proposals receiving the highest numeric value can then be ranked by importance to the congregation, and done so with confidence it expresses the congregation's sense of mission.

This does not mean other areas are less important, or that they should not be done first. Upgrading heating and cooling might be needed in order to upgrade classrooms, for instance. What this exercise does demonstrate, however, is the need to upgrade the classrooms for the congregation in order to feel it has accomplished the purpose of such a project.

Chart 2

Project Goals / Needs	Builds up people (9)	Helpful for identity (8)	Toward future church planting (7)	Spacious for growth (6)	Accessible (5)	Globally sensitive (4)	Functional (3)	On the current site (2)	Embraces change (1)	Total (#)
Renovate sanctuary		8	7	6	5		3	2	1	(31)
Update kitchen		8		6	5		3	2		(24)
Expand parking			7	6	5		3	2		(23)
Update heating and cooling				6			3	2		(11)
Move and expand church offices	9			6	5		3	2	1	(26)
Renovate classrooms	9	8			5	4	3	2	1	(32)
Move and expand parlor	9	8	7		5		3	2		(33)

Chart 3

Mission / Activities	Guided by God's call	Joyous sign of God's healing and hope: worshipful and joyous	Expresses faith and love through service in our community	Expresses faith through service at home	Expresses faith through service at work	Expresses faith through service in the world
Sunday school	*					
Worship	*	*				
Men's basketball			*			
Women's gathering				*		
Mothers of preschool children	*	*	*	*	*	*
Aerobics	*	*	*		*	
Food pantry	*		*			
Children's night			*			
Alcoholics Anonymous	*		*			
High school youth worship	*	*				

Chart 3, page 106

Notes for chart 3: For congregations that need to decide what core activities are central to its sense of mission, chart 3 can be a useful tool. The mission statement is again broken down into columns across the top of the chart. The left side lists the activities in which the congregation engages. Those filling out the chart, note their perceptions of where these items intersect with the mission statement.

Compiling these perceptions gives congregational leadership a sense of what programs are unnecessary, which critical activities need to be improved in order for the congregation to better achieve its mission, and which ones are critical to the congregation's sense of mission.

These three charts prepare the congregation for a substantive conversation before embarking on any expansion project that creates new limits for the congregation. Such a conversation is critical to success and health. The conversation needs to be sensitive to those who will live longest with the results of any decision. This conversation is not the responsibility of the Steering Committee for a project once it is underway, but the core leadership of the congregation before any project is designed.[1] A congregation that is thorough in its process—before breaking any ground—is far more ready to take on needed renovation, expansion, or new program initiatives that require modifying facilities.

When a well-planned project follows a substantive conversation like this, there is a good chance the congregation's generosity will surpass the results of any feasibility study. A good process results in a project with a price reflecting what the congregation perceives to be God's work, rather than the pet project of a few leaders.

Endowments

As the North American population continues to age, there will be a significant increase in the number of estates and their monetary distributions. Tragically, this isn't because a greater percentage of the population leaves bequests, but because there is an increasing number of elderly persons in the general population.

Some church workers are enthusiastic about endowments, while others are lukewarm or even opposed to them. Those who are against endowments in the church often argue that churches are to operate on faith, not on orders from dead people. But this argument should logically lead them to oppose estate planning for income during retirement years. They should tear up their wills too, for wills are also instructions from dead people!

Three guidelines for churches and endowments:

1. Endowments should enhance the giving potential rather than replace it. If you plan to endow something, **endow operational expenses like building maintenance, or undergird people development** through scholarship programs or foundations. Don't endow staff salaries, mission, or program. It cuts off the opportunity for the congregation to be financially involved in the congregation's operations, and it perpetuates a meet-the-budget mentality. Keep endowment reports separate from a congregation's giving estimates and spending plan.

2. A congregation is wise to **develop a policy on endowment** before someone wants to give them one. It's easier to make healthy decisions when no outside pressure is forcing the issue.

3. **Minimize endowment restrictions**. The more general the intent for an endowment's use, the longer it is able to meet needs. For instance, what would an endowment earmarked for scholarships at Windwhistle Camp do if the camp closes? It is better to designate the endowment as scholarships for summer camping, and let the endowment's trustees determine spending policies.

Endowments can be a useful tool, but only if they fuel future giving. Each generation needs to develop ownership for its congregation's mission. Financial involvement achieves this ownership if endowments don't remove the opportunity.

Long-term endowments should average 5 percent per year in distributions if they intend to remain solvent throughout prosperous and lean times. Time-limited endowment, of course, will want to distribute more. Good ethics require that expenses in maintaining an endowment are not to be exorbitant, nor interfere with the ability to make the distributions each year.

Address these three issues when establishing and using endowments:

1. Instead of debating whether endowments show or don't show faith in God, call people to a lifestyle that embraces Jubilee—returning wealth to the community for fresh and creative uses.

2. Does this endowment provide seed money for ministry dreams of younger and newer church members? Does this endowment allow someone to retain financial control long after death, or does it share responsibility for funding and financial decision making?

3. Does our desire for endowment sound as if the church will cease without one?

Notes

1. For assistance in group decision making or working with a capital campaign, contact MMA's Stewardship Education Center at 800-348-7468 or write to: stewardship@mma-online.org.
2. Ibid.

CHAPTER 9

Communicating about money management

Tips for the discussion

Here is where we tackle that age-old debate about what is good and what is not good to spend money on. Some tips for leading the conversation about how the church manages God's money follow.

Take the long view

Ask first "What are the important values of the congregation?" Money serves the values, not the other way around. Short-term decisions must not damage the long-term integrity of the congregation. State the values **every single time** a money decision is being reported or debated.

Example 1: "Because we are a congregation who engages in community service, we decided to always devote 5 percent of our spending plan to several community organizations. That is why you see an increase for the second harvest food bank."

Example 2: "It is our tradition to bless our staff for the many hours they minister on our behalf. We want their families to be strong and we want them to serve us well for many years. Thus, we are putting in place a family travel allowance for all those who are away thirty nights a year."

Speak accurately

- If you don't know the answer, say so, and immediately describe how you will find out.
- What answers you *do* have are often better conveyed in percentages than in amounts. A percentage description provides a way for everyone to understand—those who work with large amounts of money, and those who do not. A percent is a number out of 100. An amount does not easily convey the same idea.
- Instead of: "We are adding $500 to the office equipment line this year."
  Say: "We need to add 3 percent to the office equipment line because we have added extra staff with additional equipment for them to use and that we anticipate maintenance costs to be higher."
- Do not intentionally massage the facts—put a spin on them—so that members cannot see the entire picture. It will bring great trouble in the end.

Describe the issue(s) before proposing the idea

- A little background helps people understand the line of thinking and avoids forming first impressions too quickly.
- Leading with the issue before the idea also puts the suggested proposal into a less threatening and less vulnerable position as suggestions and responses are given.
- If you have an outside presenter, he or she also benefits from a description of the decision-making process. Presenters can better serve others when they also look through the window of the congregation's experience.

Income and distribution need to show connection to mission

Remember a budget alternative is the **narrative-spending plan**—the *story* of what a congregation expects to do in the giving year. A church might use its mission statement to describe what it will do:

1. Proclaim the reign of God in worship.
2. Proclaim the reign of God through ministry.
3. Proclaim the reign of God through community life.

In writing a narrative-spending plan, a story for the upcoming year, the congregation estimates the costs of accomplishing these goals, and allocates the money to make it happen. The spending plan bases financial management on distributing funds in ministry and reporting on the results ahead of the need to get more income from the congregation. It focuses on opportunity rather than getting. It connects people to the mission. It allows the staff to demonstrate the importance of each task to the congregation.

Specifics about money management and communication
Income and expense

Emphasize distribution and how it achieves a mission purpose. Many congregations and organizations use the church bulletin or newsletter to report weekly or monthly income. Then, once a year, a summary of how the money was used is reported.

Reverse this. Make the regular statement demonstrate mission uses of contributed money. Emphasize the outflow to achieve goals, rather than on the income statement. Once a year, then, issue an income statement as part of your final report.

(For examples of an invitation to estimated giving, a letter for those who did not return their pledge, and a letter confirming an estimate, see pp. 123-124 of Teaching a Christian View of Money.*)*

Here is a sample of a year's worth of quarterly membership letters from a stewardship commission:

First quarter mailing

"The Lord has done great things for us, and we rejoiced" (Psalm 126:3).

Giving to God's work is a joyful act of worship. In giving, we respond to the grace we receive from God. Through giving we declare our love to God, and show our trust in God's provision. In our worship services, ___(church name)___ Church provides many ways to participate in this worship act.

Just as it is right to return the first and best of our lives to God, we aspire to be a firstfruits congregation. From the first and best that you bring, we intend to give our first gifts beyond the needs of our congregation.

The general fund

The general fund is the largest and most significant area of giving and distribution. From it we give our congregation's firstfruits gifts to worldwide and local mission efforts, show generosity to our staff, cover the costs of holding more than one hundred worship events a year, pay for the curricula used for Christian education, and purchase supplies for our fellowship events. We are working to build a small cash reserve that helps us manage the flow of our gifts.

The building fund

Our recently built facilities grew out of our vision to worship God and bring a presence of Jesus into our surrounding neighborhood. We are engaged in the ambitious goal of paying off our mortgage within five years by (year). Contributions to the building fund need to be designated on your check or offering envelope.

Love funds

We have a variety of funds for extending God's love and mercy. In contributing to these funds, you must designate it on your check or giving envelope. Love funds include:

- **Mutual aid fund.** The purpose of this fund is to carry out mutual aid within our membership: and secondarily, to meet community needs.
- **Aid to widows and orphans.** This fund assists families who temporarily or permanently lose family members.
- **Revolving loan fund:** A revolving loan fund for high-risk situations. This fund is available to members and regular attendees. The purpose of this fund is to provide assistance at low interest rates for people who have special needs at special times.
- **Seminary education fund.** This fund assists seminary students that are completing their education.
- **Short-term mission fund.** From time to time someone in our congregation participates in a short-term mission assignment. This fund helps us assist with the expenses of the one(s) serving.

Additional perspective

Giving is an act of worship and praise to God. To help you experience this; we invite you to bring all your giving to church on Sunday.

When making a contribution to a charity, just place the gift in an addressed envelope with appropriate postage and place it in the offering plate. In this way, we can bless all our giving to God and praise God for the blessings we receive. Gifts given in this way are mailed following worship by our church staff. Receipts will come to you from the receiving agency.

- To help you keep record of your giving and for claiming the tax benefit, ___(church name)___ Church provides giving envelopes. Simply request them from the church office. You will receive a quarterly report of your giving and updates on our ministry with your gifts.
- Finally, some financial institutions allow you to give electronically. One benefit from electronic fund transfers (EFT) is that giving is truly a firstfruits act. If this is your desire, please contact the church office for routing numbers. We also encourage you to keep an offering envelope in which you can place your transfer receipts and continue to participate in worship offerings.

Second quarter mailing

One way the___[church]___ family has celebrated the start of a new year is by increased giving. Overall income is up by ____[percent], helping us continue giving the first and best of our congregation's income, while trusting in God's provision. We have also generously responded to the need for replenishing our mutual aid fund. This is something to celebrate! (Explain how community ministries are being funded.)

We want to continue moving away from "we have-to-meet-the-budget" attitudes toward a spending plan that assumes we will use the gifts we receive for ministry that exalts God. Further we want to continue cultivating giving as an act of worshipful trust in God, rather than simply a funding mechanism. Introduced just last year is the idea that you can give any gifts through the offering, and [church name] will mail them for you. (Include an addressed/stamped envelope with your gift.) In this way you can begin offering these gifts for God's purposes, as you would your regular giving, through [church name]. Another new feature is the monthly income and distribution statement in the bulletin. If you have other ideas to help us move toward more worshipful and celebrative giving, we invite you to talk with a Stewardship Commission member.

Here's an update on [church name] financial status:

You may be interested to know that we consider our utility costs a ministry expense, not just mere overhead. A chief activity of [church name] is the 100 + worship services each year, 26 or more "Evenings at Church," and the many community ministries happening every night of the week. When we use the lights, heat the building, and run the water, we do it in order to worship God and serve others. Our utility costs truly are God-directed.

As we enter the second quarter of giving, dedicating these gifts, then distributing them for God's use, may God bless you and grant you grace after grace.

The Stewardship Commission

Third quarter mailing

We are now six months into our year of worship and ministry. We have heard stories of commitment to a relationship with our Lord, shared in baptismal vows, prayed for healing, and celebrated the resurrection of Jesus. We shared meals, tutored children, refereed at basketball games, visited the sick, studied the Scriptures, called [name] as our pastor, invited friends and family to join us in worship, assisted evangelism and service efforts around the world, met in cluster groups, and recently

celebrated _____. Our congregational life is rich
with opportunity for worship, fellowship, and ministry.

This year we decided to spend $297,007 in accom-
plishing our ministry goals. Of that amount, $77,295 or
26 percent we intend to give to broader ministries
beyond our congregation as our corporate firstfruits worship of God.

As of the end of the second quarter, $130,858 was
dedicated to the Lord's work in our worship services. In
addition to money used for our staff, facilities, and ministries, we distributed $28,015 or 21 percent to broader
ministries like the education, missions. Congregational
members,   _____,   _____,
_____, and _____ represent our con-
gregation in sharing the gospel around the world.

The attached statement shows your estimate of firstfruits giving for the year, as well as your giving for the
first six months of the year. We are grateful for your gifts.

The Stewardship Commission gratefully acknowledges the many ways people contribute to our rich congregational life. We also thank God for the many members who carry the Spirit of Christ into their homes, voca-
tions, and involvement in the boarder community.
Finally, please keep us informed on ways we can best
serve you as a commission. We want to enhance the many
joys of giving, and enrich your life as stewards of God's
many gifts.

Fourth quarter mailing

Greetings in the name of our Lord Jesus Christ. Our
year, _(year)_ is now three-fourths gone. Recent weeks
brought funerals, births, weddings, and the start of a new
Sunday school year. Our community ministries continue
to grow and we are now looking ahead to the results of
our strategic planing. Central to all this activity is our

worship of God and our love for each other.

Our income and planned expenses are based on your promised giving. This income and the related expenses help us accomplish our stated goals. It also helps us weather the unexpected challenges that come when nearly 200 people consider this their congregation. One specific goal for the $297,007 we plan to receive is to give 26 percent of our funds ($77,295) to share in ministry and mission with other congregations around the world.

By the end of the third quarter, $205,712 was brought to (name of congregation) as the worship response of our congregation. We have been able to continue this worship by passing along $37,330 or 18% to those wider ministries. In addition, we distributed $20,034 from our various mutual aid funds this year. A brochure detailing those funds is available (where). We anticipate being at 26% by year's end. During the next fiscal year we will work at building a stronger cash reserve that enables us to be more consistent with our congregation's generosity throughout the year.

On behalf of the entire congregation, the Stewardship Commission thanks you for the contributions you make from week to week. We want your gifts to be used for God's glory, and we want to manage them so your excitement for giving is heightened.

May God bless you, keep you, and meet you in the middle of your needs and opportunities.

When giving exceeds expectation

Many organizations and congregations are reluctant to move from a position of scarcity—to be flush, to have anything left over, or to develop operating reserves—for fear they show they don't have faith, or that they are greedy, or that they are not accomplishing their goals. It is reasonable to set a small operating reserve that reflects a percentage of the annual income.

Some congregations won't need more than 7-10 percent; others who operate schools or large scholarship funds out of operating expenses, often need as much as 25 percent or more. When the reserve rises above the maximum, the organization *rushes* to distribute it. When the reserve falls below the minimum, it triggers a protection to build it up again in the next fiscal year. In the meantime the reserve is used to help the congregation meet its goals for the current year. In this way, the congregation or organization is better equipped to fulfill its mission on any given day of the year, and has a policy in place for dealing with shortages and overages, instead of needing to deal with it on a case by case basis.

In addition, any overage is an occasion to celebrate!

Sample proposal regarding excess income:

(Year) was another tremendous year of giving at (name of church). Our total offerings and receipts exceed actual disbursements by $26,350. We praise God for that! After much prayer, discussion, reflection, and consultation the Stewardship Commission proposes the following:

1. **Send 20 percent of surplus to missions and agencies now.** This 20 percent is the missions and agencies percentage of our total spending plan.
2. **Establish a cash reserve.** A cash reserve will help our congregation manage funds as income ebbs and flows. This is better than using mission dollars to manage these ebbs and flows by not meeting our planned commitments in years when giving fell short. A cash reserve is a mechanism to even out our various disbursements. In months when

giving is a little higher, money is set aside above expenses to replenish the reserve. In months when giving shrinks, the reserve keeps a steady cash flow. If the cash reserve needs to be replenished, an amount will be built into the spending plan for the coming year.

Establishing a cash reserve helps us become a firstfruits congregation. With the cash reserve, as well as quarterly special mission offerings, we can distribute money more consistently to missions and agencies throughout the year, rather than giving the majority at the end of the year. While the reserve will be a tool to manage our giving, we will not let it exceed 5 percent of the current year's spending plan. A joyful decision regarding distribution of the excess over 5 percent would be made *by the governing body of the congregation.*

3. **Always meet the missions commitment**. With the help of a generous congregation, we agree to always fully fund our annual commitment to the missions and agencies. If the need arose, we would access a line of credit to meet our various obligations. We say "missions" is important, but to be willing to access a line of credit to meet our commitment says loud and clear how critically important that commitment really is to us! Accessing this line of credit would be a last resort if our income does not meet our commitments.

When there is a shortfall

Horrible catastrophe? The more important question is whether the annual goals were achieved. If they were, celebrate! If not, blaming and pleading are of no use, and may even hinder future growth. Be frank in reporting the financial state of affairs, but stay focused on the goals that *are* being achieved.

Also, don't give in to across-the-board cuts of minimal amounts. A slow death by trimming is not the answer. Instead, evaluate whether it would be wise to invite others to participate in the goals of the organization or congregation. It is also now time to investigate whether all the activities, programs, and committees help the organization achieve its purpose. If not, drop them in favor of those that do.

These conversations are occasions for leaders to state publicly the agreed-upon goals, and the long-term view for the organization. Without doing so, the process degenerates into political lobbying.

Sample letter from a congregation that is experiencing shortfall

The year _____ has special significance for church. It was in 1874, 125 years ago, that Mennonite settlers came to this area. We have so much for which to be thankful! Over the years church has had strong leadership. Many programs and ministries of this congregation have met the needs of countless people.

- As the year closes, here are some highlights. Our pastoral leadership:
- Baptized seventeen people on Pentecost Sunday
- Affirmed the youth minister for another three years
- Attended area and churchwide conferences (name them)
- Traveled to youth conference with a busload of youth
- Walked with families in grief and following a personal loss
- Continued to challenge the congregation to a more intimate relationship with God, through

sound preaching and counseling
- Continued the strong network of support through prayer and visitation
- [other specifics]

We began two new life-giving ministries this year:
- The deacons and elders, together with the pastors, recognized a need for more attention directed to prayer in the lives of individuals and in the life of the church. A resource for this prayer ministry is _____(name)_____, who is leading and training volunteers to be sources of support and encouragement to members of our church.
- _____ has been working in lay ministry, focusing on building a young adult ministry.

The Board of Business Administration continues to do an excellent job of monitoring and maintaining our worship facility. With the use of designated estate funds the process of replacing courtyard doors and windows continues. As funds become available we will do a major repair to the underside of the sanctuary roof.

At the end of September our giving was up $4,350 compared to last year at that time. This is wonderful news! With the money we were able to encourage local projects such as the newly formed preschool, offer a variety of Sunday school options to adults, provide literature on "What Mennonites Believe," host a family blessing workshop on Valentine's Day weekend, host a workshop on church planting, complete funds for the west stained-glass window, and add to the roofing fund.

Our church supported ministries outside the congregation also. Money given to missions and service has been used to support missionaries and service workers such as (names). Offerings received for education trains leaders and provides the congregation with study materials. (denominational missionary training administration) trains pastors and missionaries from around the world. Our congregation benefits from association with the Northern District and supports area church planting such as New Hope Mennonite Church in (name of city/area). (Church name) exists to make disciples both at home and in the broader world.

Being faithful in our home congregation includes paying pastoral and support staff salaries. The situation is that much of the generosity has gone to support special projects, leaving the operating budget in a $41,000 deficit. This amount is being borrowed from special project funds and will need to be replaced. Our giving to other causes such mission, conference, and church schools have also decreased by approximately $34,000. We have been overspending the church operating receipts and underspending the budget. When this occurs, we find that many worthwhile projects, both here at home and also the broader church don't receive adequate support. Our local facilities and programs suffer as well as mission programs outside church name.

It is an important, challenging, but attainable goal to have church name finish the year in the black. It will be a challenge, but a very achievable goal, especially when one considers the many ways God has blessed us. It is important that every member respond generously in the remaining fiscal year. Our responses to God financially, in time and service, are indicators of our relationship to God.

When something is expensive

When the congregation needs to buy something necessary, not frivolous, yet expensive, all the skills listed here come to bear. Set the context. Lead with the issues. Take the long view. Speak accurately. Be ready to absorb and acknowledge anxiety. A word of caution is that something expensive should not be undertaken if a change of leadership is imminent.

"Tainted" money

With a lot of money changing hands between generations, with the increasing wealth in some sectors in society, and with the increasing amount of funding required by the local congregation, some ministry leaders may face ethical issues about the origins of money that comes to them.

Some refuse any donation of dubious origin. They say they will rely on God to find the money from more pure sources. Others take Martin Luther's attitude: "Let God have it. The devil's had it long enough."

Both approaches are right. We don't want to rely on the largesse of individuals, corporations, or governments given over to sin. Neither do we want to operate as if our God can't redeem money. If God can't redeem money, how can God redeem us?

If we are effective in ministering to people, there will be Zacchaeuses in our congregations—people who convert from an old pattern into a new one, and who will want to use previously corrupted money in holy ways. When this happens, the church needs a consistent ethic from which to operate. Here is one suggestion: **church leaders should act as brokers when redeeming corrupted money.**

Don't bypass the opportunity to minister to people who wish to give corrupted money, even if the donation is a futile attempt to relieve a troubled conscience. This is an occasion to speak directly and with love. The only way this can be done, however, is if the speaker is not on the receiving end of the donation—personally or for the ministry organization they represent. This is where the work of church foundations can help.

For example: Peter Bordreau won $15,000 in the lottery and wanted to donate half of it to his church. But the pastor was on public record as opposing the lottery. Instead of accepting these funds for the church, the pastor helped Peter make an anonymous donation to a different charity. The money was no longer used for selfish purposes, the pastor had integrity when talking to Peter about the need to give all the proceeds away and to stop playing the lottery, and a worthy charity benefited without the potential of undue influence. This solution redeemed money and preserved integrity.

Fear that money will be misused

What happens when trust breaks down, especially when it concerns church funds? We want to be generous, but what if we are afraid that someone will misuse what we intended for God's work? What should be done when someone embezzles church funds? Should Christians stop giving to organizations, and only give to individuals who have demonstrated their integrity? May it never be!

Giving exclusively to specific organizations and individuals means we cease giving in worship. It means we cease celebrating God's generosity in the presence of our sisters and brothers. It means we stop publicly declaring we have only one God. It means we cease dedicating wealth for God's purposes. God is the final arbiter of wealth. Whether money is embezzled, stolen, misused, or foolishly wasted, God's use of that money is not ruined. Ultimately our giving is about showing who our God is, and giving what is most precious to us in worship. We can give in faith that money dedicated to God's purposes will eventually get there, no matter how far of the track it may get.

CHAPTER 10

Planning for change

Getting people to accept change

Growth requires change. You need to know how individuals will likely respond to your initiatives. When a change process begins, a congregation will quickly discover that it has the following four groups of people:

- **Enthusiastic supporters** (5-15% of the congregation)—These people jump in early, with lots of energy. They vocally support the process, volunteer their gifts, and help build additional support. They often perceive that they have the most to gain from a change process.
- **Supporters** (35-45%)—These people generally support the process, are willing for church leaders and others to give their time to it, and will often ask questions to get more information. They may be unclear about the benefits of the process, but they trust choices made by congregational leadership, as long as it is open and accountable.
- **Cautious** (35-45%)—These people prefer that conversations about the change process be kept on a theoretical level—especially if it means they can avoid making a commitment. While their support can be slowly cultivated as they see the process succeeding, they can also withdraw support quickly.
- **Opposed** (5-15%)—This group has significant

questions about the process, and may never give support to it. They need to know they are valued, that their concerns were sincerely considered, and maybe even used to improve the overall process. They also need to know that leadership is firmly and lovingly committed to proceed. Take them seriously, but don't let them defeat the process of change!

Keep track of the relative size of each of the four groups as the process continues. If the process is led by patient and mature people; if the process is informative, relaxed and accountable; if questions are answered and any opposition is thoroughly listened to, the enthusiastic and supportive groups will be larger at the end of a change process than at the beginning.

On the other hand, if the process is uptight and impatient; if leadership fails to provide adequate information, or ceases to listen; if the process is disconnected from a deep spiritual source, opposition will solidify. Cautious people will align themselves with those already opposed, supportive people will become cautious, and enthusiastic people will disappear.

Another, slightly different, way to view how you can expect people to change is as follows (*Leadership*, spring 1999):

- **Innovators** (2%) Not usually policy makers.
- **Early adopters** (18%) Respected and influential, they know a good idea when they see it.
- **Middle adopters** (60%) They react to ideas rather than generate their own. If you convince this group, your idea will probably "sell." They support status quo unless you give them a good reason to change, or are assured that change won't result in loss of quality.

- **Late adopters** (18%) While they will speak against change, they will probably go along with it if the majority goes the new way.
- **Never adopters** (2%) Committed to the past, they may either disrupt if they don't get their way, or leave.

Em Griffin in *The Mind Changers* (Tyndale House, 1981, p. 228) likens the stages of change to the stages of candle making.

- *Melt*: Soften resistance to change through patient and loving service.
- *Mold*: Shape gradually and carefully when seeking long-lasting change.
- *Make hard*: Put together external and internal supports to make change permanent.

Strategies for dealing with negative and counterproductive response to change

- Set a time to listen to objections and clarify so that those who oppose know they were heard. Do not defend proposed change.
- Use conciliatory speech, avoid harsh rhetoric.
- Find an objective facilitator (this helps people become part of the change process).
- Be willing for proposed change to reflect the ideas of those who oppose it.

What *doesn't* work:

- Getting defensive
- Giving advice: "What I would do if I were you . . ."
- Persuading prematurely
- Censoring: cutting a person out of discussion
- Controlling: making a power play to be sure your way wins

- Punishing those who oppose the change by not letting them share in its benefits
- Becoming resigned with an "Oh, well" attitude

Re-covering tradition

Take a really old chair. It's got nicks in the paint, worn cushions, a loose leg. Ready to become firewood? No. It has been passed down in your family for generations. You aren't going to burn the tradition now. But you also can't let the decay continue, or you'll have nothing to pass down.

Garry Wills says that in order for a tradition to be worth passing to another generation that you must "restore it to its original state or condition." Or you must "repristinate" it—a term used in an interview with worship leader Joseph Garlington (*Leadership*, spring 1999). This means action, not leaving something alone. If you leave it completely alone, it disintegrates. Like recovering the chair that was neglected in the interests of preserving its antiquity, one has to do a lot to something to bring it back to its once pristine condition, not just leave it alone. Leaving it alone doesn't mean it won't change; it still changes, by rotting away. A tradition is like that. It needs continual interpretation/explanation, in short repristination.

Repristination is the reason some songs from earlier times catch on again. A hymn can maintain its freshness if you keep that hymn exposed to fresh expressions. For example, leading worship is more about *modeling* worship, by being the lead worshiper, not by telling worshipers what to do, but by doing it and giving them permission to do what you do. A lead worshiper's job is to recognize the moment, and then point others to it; the grace gates. A church leader's job with money is the same: model firstfruits living, and seize those moments that give others permission to do it too.

Most church leaders know how to convince people to try something new in worship: Let children lead. How do we do that with money matters? "Growing up" in the reign of God doesn't mean we are required to become more reserved. Maturity isn't being stiffer. It's becoming less focused on myself and more aware of who God is. Make the goal not to get people to do things they haven't done before. Make the goal helping people worship by giving. Usually the best way to move people to worship through giving is to see leaders worshiping God that way.

Still, leaders need to be gentle with people who are slow to embrace change. For example, a congregation may have worked at giving estimates for five years and seen an increase each year until the last two. It seems to have stabilized at between 70-80 percent participation. The congregation can expect those who do not participate to give the same amount they did the previous year. It also needs to vary the methods every couple of years to maintain interest. And though many participated in giving estimates, they weren't always quick to follow through. The leadership now sends a quarterly thank-you for people's giving. These notes combine the record of their giving with what the church has seen God do with their monetary worship. By being systematic and sending thank-yous to *everyone* whether they are behind or exceeding their giving, the church doesn't single anyone out and continues the positive spirit they care so much about. The result: an improvement in follow-through.

French priest Teilhard de Chardin said, "We're not just human beings having a temporary human existence. We're spiritual beings having a temporary human experience."

Tap the royal priesthood

Christians stand in the tradition of the royal priest-hood. We are both kings and priests. We rule with God, in God's way. We are like priestly intermediaries, pointing the way to God, upholding what God has envisioned. And just as the king and priest were anointed to identify them with God's service, we too participate in an act of consecration—water baptism. In baptism we join this nation of kingly priests who are set apart for God's purposes.

Those who know they are part of a kingdom of priests ask, Who can I bless? For whom can I pray? Who can I disciple? Who can I prepare to fill my role when I am gone? How will I let others lead me? How can I help others find their home in the church?

This change in identity can change a congregation's behavior as well. Here are at least four corporate behavioral changes that take place:

1. **They drop a program orientation and move into a gifting orientation.** Instead of saying, "We need a Sunday school teacher for the second and third graders, would you do it?" They start saying, "We're glad to have you as a part of us. We would like to know what your ministering gifts are, and how you would like to be involved." Churches like this understand the saying, "We get people done through things, not things done through people."

2. **They are concerned about healthy decision-making environments.** They think the most critical step in the future health of their church is how future leaders are called. They make sure those who do the calling are given adequate resources for training those they call. They take plenty of time in worship and prayer when choices must be made. They measure the success of their decisions on whether

it seemed good to them and to the Holy Spirit rather than on whether it was particularly expedient and efficient. They use business tools and good process skills, but only as they serve the discernment process, not as ends in themselves. They understand that the work of committees is not to preserve past methods, but to lead into the future.

3. **They become expansive instead of only inclusive.** Inclusion is one of today's buzzwords, but beyond being inclusive, a truly royal priesthood is expansive. Inclusion assumes someone retains the power to involve someone else. Expansion means someone is willing to share power or give it up altogether.

   Expansive people listen to what others care about, even when they disagree. Those who are expansive go beyond creating room in their life for someone else. They are also willing to adjust their life to accommodate the newcomer. Instead of saying, "You are welcome to come here, especially if you appreciate all that we do." They say, "How can we create a new future together?" At the same time, expansive people are not wishy-washy. They do not drop convictions for the sake of relationships. Neither do they drop relationships for the sake of convictions. They remain firmly planted on the gospel message, but follow the example of the Shepherd who seeks out all the sheep.

4. **They extend God's reign.** Because they know they are a royal priesthood, they pray unceasingly for God's direction. They want to see effective discipleship and Christian education as a cornerstone of the ministry of their church. They care about expanding God's peace, justice, and abundance around the world.

If we live out our royal priesthood by pointing the way to God, then we grow disciples to continue the work of Jesus. With a royal priesthood orientation we can discard ineffective methods without remorse. The goal is not to get a new Christian to write a check to the church. The goal is to help a new Christian find such a deep love for Jesus, that all of his or her life belongs to God, including the new Christian's checkbook.

Appendix A

Stewardship definitions

The perspective of *Speaking About Money* is that stewardship at its highest and best form is found in worship of God. Accordingly then, the commonly used stewardship terms take on new meaning. The following are key terms and their definitions as found in this volume.

Steward: Someone who organizes life so God can give them away.

Stewardship: Organizing life so God can give you away.

Stewardship education: Helping others organize life so God can give them away.

Firstfruits: First *and* best. The prime of what one is given or what one produces. Firstfruits refer to the portion set aside as a worshipful response to the God who caresses the whole world.

Firstfruits living: Offering the first and best of life to God in worship, and using the rest in generous ways that honor God.

Tithe: A starting point for proportionally giving one's first and best. For those observing the law of Moses, a tithe referred to a 10-percent portion of the harvest, or the income produced if a harvest was sold. Presentation of the tithe took place at the temple as an act of worship. As Western society shifted from an agricultural to a monetary economy, many Christian traditions carried forward the expectation of the tithe as 10 percent of gross household income, again as a gift to be presented in worship, usually through the local congregation. However, many remain unaware that the Hebrews presented a tithe twice and sometimes three times in a year.

The instruction of Jesus is that tithing must be done in conjunction with a deep concern for justice, mercy, and faithfulness (Matthew 23:23) or it becomes meaningless. Thus, the concept of first-fruits living, as defined above, is more solidly aligned with Jesus' instruction than the tithe alone. For those seeking to enforce the tithe, or seeking to abandon it, 10 percent of income is the limit of stewardship responsibility. A firstfruits lifestyle, however, finds it is only the beginning.

Offering: Giving beyond a tithe. Offerings are usually more spontaneous and less systematic than giving of a tithe, but still are given in worship settings.

Charitable gift: In formal terms, a charitable gift is a gift of money or asset to any not-for-profit organization. The organization then issues a receipt that the donor can use in filing for a tax deduction. In less formal use, a charitable gift can mean any act of "charity," that is, showing mercy to others. While most tithes and offerings can be considered charitable gifts, they are not synonymous.

Jubilee: A year of celebration for the Hebrew people every fifty years (Leviticus 25). Debts were to be canceled and land ownership was to be restored. Most Christian traditions understand this to be a permanent way of living now that Jesus, the Messiah, has come (compare Luke 4:14-19). How this is lived out in a capitalist society is the subject of much conversation between Christians, with no easy answers. Many Christians refer to the list of ministries in Luke 4 (preaching good news to the poor, proclaiming freedom for prisoners, bringing recovery of sight for the blind, and releasing the oppressed) as the methods of Jubilee. Others point to the distribution of the family estate, saying it should be made available to more than one's biological heirs. Others make periods of Jubilee an opportunity to return to God and find God's forgiveness. If stewardship is first and foremost an act of worship, however, then the celebration of God's provision becomes the focal point of Jubilee. The Christian learns to rejoice in any opportunity to declare trust in God's provision, or to dance upon injustice.

Appendix B

Index of terms

Appendix C

Selected bibliography

Bonder, Rabbi Nilton, *The Kabbalah of Money*, Boston: Shambalah Press, 1996, 176 pp.

Callahan, Kennon L., *Giving and Stewardship in an Effective Church: A Guide for Every Member*, HarperSanFrancisco, 1992, 132 pp.

Callahan, Kennon L., *Effective Church Finances: Fund-raising and Budgeting for Church Leaders*, HarperSanFrancisco, 1992, 166 pp.

Ellul, Jacques, *Money and Power*, Downers Grove: InterVarsity Press, 1984, 173 pp.

Getz, Gene A., *A Biblical Theology of Material Possessions*, Chicago: Moody Press, 1990, 438 pp.

Hershberger, Michele, *A Christian View of Hospitality: Expecting Surprises*, Scottdale: Herald Press, 1999, 284 pp.

Miller, Lynn A., *Firstfruits Living: Giving God Our Best*, Scottdale: Herald Press, 1991, 96 pp.

Moore, Gary, *Ten Golden Rules for Financial Success*, Grand Rapids: Zondervan, 1996, 198 pp.

Ray, David R., *The Big Small Church Book*, Cleveland: Pilgrim Press, 1992, 233 pp.

Vincent, Mark, *A Christian View of Money: Celebrating God's Generosity*, Scottdale: Herald Press, 1997, 136 pp.

Vincent, Mark, *Teaching a Christian View of Money: Celebrating God's Generosity*, Scottdale: Herald Press, 1997, 134 pp.

Vincent, Mark, *A Stewardship Manifest*, pdf file from www.GivingProject.net, 2000, 30 pp.

Vincent, Waldo J., *Christian Stewards: Confronted and Committed*, St. Louis: Concordia Publishing House, 1982, 186 pp.

About the author

Mark Vincent lives near Milwaukee, Wisconsin, with his wife, Lorie, and their two children, Autumn and Zach. Mark leads Design for Ministry, a creative contracting and consulting firm that helps ministry organizations and congregations accomplish their goals.

In addition to youth ministry, urban pastoral experience, and retreat center program leadership, Mark pioneered work in neighborhood ministry to children, congregational leadership development and decision-making, The Giving Project, Stewardship University sponsored by Mennonite Mutual Aid (Goshen, Indiana), and other unique stewardship events that benefit congregations.

Vincent, a frequent speaker and lecturer, is known for his story-telling. His education includes a B.A. in biblical studies from Fort Wayne (Ind.) Bible College; and an M.A. in ministry from Moody Bible Institute, Chicago, Illinois. Additional theological and management studies were taken at Associated Mennonite Biblical Seminary,

Elkhart, Indiana, and other educational centers.

Mark is an instructor for the Christian Stewardship Association's Institute and serves as a board member of the Ecumenical Stewardship Center.

Vincent is author of *A Christian View of Money: Celebrating God's Generosity, Teaching a Christian View of Money, Untold Stories of Advent, The Art of Agreement, Congregational Diagnostics,* and *A Stewardship Manifest.* He has written stewardship curricula and contributed to several church magazines. Mark currently edits *Giving* magazine for the Ecumenical Stewardship Center.

Mark's interests include reading broadly, particularly fiction, biographies, ancient history, and from various business disciplines. He also enjoys making music, body surfing, urban hiking, and eating in new restaurants. Vincent is an ordained minister with Mennonite Church USA.